$7\overset{50}{8}$

Martha Ann Walker
846 Monticello Rd —
, appa.

Humor
in American Song

HUMOR
in American Song

By ARTHUR LOESSER

ARRANGEMENTS BY ALFRED KUGEL

Illustrated by SAMUEL M. ADLER

HOWELL, SOSKIN, PUBLISHERS, NEW YORK

Manufactured entirely in the United States.

The Contents

Preface

AMERICANS LIKE TO LAUGH, AND THEY LIKE TO sing. Moreover, they like to laugh when they sing. So it is hardly surprising that in more than a century and a half of national life they have produced an enormous quantity of humorous popular songs.

This book presents a sampling of these songs, representative, it is hoped. Some of those included have been popular for a long time, and are still alive in our minds many decades after they were first brought forth. Others have been largely forgotten, but have been thought worth reviving, both for their historical as well as their intrinsic interest.

Some of these songs were first unconcernedly uttered by anonymous individuals, and were for a long time transmitted exclusively by word of mouth; others were originally set down on paper by their authors, and were to some extent, transmitted by the medium of the printed page.

No distinction has been made by the compiler between these types of songs. It has always seemed to him that the song-making impulse, like the love-making impulse, is not different when it stirs in the mind of an illiterate, than when it does so in the mind of one who can write. Nor is he impressed with the fact that verbally transmitted songs show variants from place to place and period to period, that they have "a life of their own." All songs, if they remain popular long enough, suffer transformations and developments, improvements and corruptions, whether they began with print or not. Even people who can read don't bother much to stick literally to the text when they sing for their own pleasure. Only sophisticates and pedants have any reverence for the neatness and authenticity of type.

Thus no stress has been laid on what some people call "folksong." It is not a pretty word. It is doubtful whether it is an English word at all; certainly it is not an American one. It has a very German flavor, its first half sounds like a loose adaptation of the German word "Volk." We have folks in this country, but no "folk." No one would dare name an American newspaper "The Folkish Observer." The very folks who sing "folksongs" never refer to them as that.

The word seems to carry the unpleasant suggestion that if I'm from Brooklyn, sing you a song, get it published and have it taken up and enjoyed by millions of people—that is just plain vulgar and uninteresting. But if you should hear a substantially similar sort of song in the Great Dismal Swamp, sung by a couple of hoboes with screech-owl feathers on their heads, why, that is wonderful and delightful.

The "folksong" addicts convey the scurrilous impression that they regard Brooklynites, South Siders and Mission District denizens as mere trash, whereas they consider hill-billies to be nature's noblemen. There are a lot of Brooklyners, South Siders and Mission Districtites in the country, and they can hardly be blamed if they can't quite see it that way. Hill-billies are fine in their way, but city-slicker Ph.D. hill-billy fanciers are a little less fine.

The French are pretty hard-boiled people, intellectually speaking; they don't readily get jags on German romanticist verbiage. So they have no such word or idea as "folksong." They merely speak of "chansons populaires." Popular songs are all we have in this book.

Humor has been a persistent feature of American life and utterance for a long time. The American has long been understood to be a fellow who not only likes to laugh, but is willing to be laughed at and rather enjoys laughing at himself. The article on "Humor" in the Encyclopedia Britannica has a special sub-heading entitled American Humor. American characters in foreign literature have been humorous, more often than not.

No other people seems to prize the humorous slant on all phases of life as highly as we do. Ministers of the Gospel, Chairmen of Boards of Directors and Presidents of the United States are constantly trying to spike their solemnities with comic relief, to the universal gratitude of their hearers. After-dinner speakers are usually considered successful in proportion to the number of laughs they get. Without their funny-sheets, few newspapers would keep up their circulations. Any American feels deeply ashamed at being accused of having no sense of humor. Forty years ago Broadway shows used to advertise: "50 Beautiful Girls —100 Laughs!" At that time almost any Russian would say: "What a beautiful melody! It's so sad!"

It is a little difficult to follow the course of American humor, at least in its musical aspects, back to Colonial times. Many of the songs of the people who settled and roamed the Southern hills can be traced to pre-Revolutionary times. Many of their songs are humorous. But whether the humorous ones are the real old ones seems uncertain. Evidence is lacking. It is only recently that any of them were committed to writing. Most of these songs were brought over from England and so may be called American chiefly in an inchoate sense. Yet "Sourwood Mountain" and the "Bird Song" were listed by Cecil Sharp in his monumental collection as not having been noted by any collector of songs in

England. If they can be shown to have existed in the middle of the Eighteenth century they would be about the oldest extant humorous American songs.

American humor in music seems to show more demonstrable traces along with the upsurge of the feeling for American independence. There is, for example "Yankee Doodle." A lot of inconclusive research has been done on the origin of this famous ditty; but the story most generally accepted is that its opening verse was coined in ridicule of the rustic crudities of some American troops. The Yankees enjoyed the joke on themselves and the song was an American favorite throughout the Revolution and ever since. A typical American touch, that.

For the most part, however, those humorous songs of the early days of the republic, of which both words and music have survived in print, are either of actual English origin, or are modeled closely on English patterns. Even vigorously patriotic anti-British sentiments were voiced, more often than not, to English-made tunes. Our very national anthem is an outstanding example.

This is not to say that a healthy culture of American song, purely native in the spirit of both words and music, was not already in the making at that time. But the more literate and respectable members of the population were still in the thrall of English precedent, and it was they who were the principal customers of the printing presses. "We ought to call it the War of the Revolution," said Benjamin Franklin. "The War of Independence is yet to be fought." What backwoods songs there were seemed as yet too barbarous for the publishers. Even as late as the 1830's a large proportion of the published songs had their origin in England, and their English successes were advertised as an attraction for American customers.

10

Typical American humor seems to have earned general recognition as such along with the rise and triumph of Andrew Jackson. This remarkable man became the leader of millions of people of his own sort: shrewd, crude, ignorant, ambitious, de-Europeanized frontiersmen. They expressed themselves with a vivid, irreverent realism which, however, rarely touched the depths of malice. The elation they felt at the process of building a new world extended to their speech: it abounded in savory new formations, and had nothing but disdain for the conventions of "correct" English.

Jacksonian democracy had a long sway; it formed a deep, perhaps the deepest stratum in the geology of the American soul. Millions of people in this age of aeroplanes have a nostalgia for it. The song "Great Grandad" on page 204, undoubtedly a recent composition, expresses it. Jacksonian democracy typified America as a whole to the world at large, especially to foreigners. Keen, ungrammatical, misspelled, slangy, disrespectful comment on all kinds of human doings, plus an unwillingness to be overawed by European sacred cows, became the vein of the typical American humorist, from Artemus Ward, Mark Twain and Josh Billings through Mr. Dooley, on to Will Rogers.

A new element, harmonious with the general cultural atmosphere, came into American popular entertainment at this period—that is, in the 1830's—namely the minstrel shows. Up until then American musical theaters had been chiefly occupied with ballad operas of the English type; now we find flawless Anglo-Saxons blacking up their faces, trying successfully to imitate the look, gestures, dancing, speech, voice, attitudes and manner of the lowly Negroes. These shows were pretty "low" in their general atmosphere, and polite ladies and gentlemen looked down their noses at them; but their popularity increased

11

rapidly, and perhaps even on that account. They were purely American, for one thing, and spoke a language that could hardly be called English in the dictionary sense. They were necessarily humorous, and so were most of the songs which formed an essential part of them.

The triumph of Jacksonian America (in which, of course, is included hosts of people who did not actually hold with Jackson politically) made it seem reasonable for some of these Negroesque songs to attain the dignity of print. That gave them a wide circulation, and some of the earliest ones soon passed permanently into the public consciousness and affection. It is interesting to reflect that the most famous patriotic and sentimental songs of the period ("America," "Home, Sweet, Home," and the "Star Spangled Banner") are all sung to English melodies, whereas "Jump Jim Crow" and "Zip Coon" (also known as "The Turkey in the Straw") are entirely native and vernacular.

For nearly a century the minstrel shows were one of the most fertile sources of popular humorous song. "Dixie," one of our most inspiring melodies, was originally a minstrel "walk around." Many of Stephen Foster's most famous and beloved tunes were baptized in burnt cork.

There were other fountains of song. Traveling troupes, such as the Hutchinsons, made the rounds of the cities and brought new songs to increasing multitudes of people. Some these had a less broad, primitive humor than those of the minstrels, their language was somewhat closer to "proper" English. Many of them were topical, that is, they dealt with special events and conditions of the day. The humorous aspects of fashionable crazes were dealt with, of political situations, of women's foibles, of the accents of immigrants, the tightness of money, the oil speculation fever. Some of the songs were, indeed, aimed at a rather well-bred market, and had a kind of lady-like quality.

Even the Civil War, with its harvest of death and anguish, inspired a few humorous songs. One of the best was "Kingdom Comin'," expressing the supposed joy of Southern negroes when their masters were called away.

After the war, foreign immigrants, especially Germans and Irish, were a conspicuous feature of the lives of our cities. Their struggles with American diction were an unfailing source of popular laughter. Harrigan and Hart, favorite pair of comedians, entertained a couple of decades of Americans with funny songs, promulgated in Irish dialect.

Meanwhile a lot of songs were produced among special groups of people, suited to the particular circumstances of their lives. Largely anonymous, they were in any case innocent of the idea of commercial exploitation. Occupational groups developed their own songs: the cowboys sang of their ropings and herdings, the anthracite coal miners of the details of their jobs, the sailors of theirs, likewise the lumberjacks and the railroad workers. Many of these songs dealt with the hardships of life, but many turned out humorous just the same. Tough work, hard times, injustice, risk of limb and even death could all be laughed at by Americans. College boys gave vent to their youthful exuberance in songs, many of them with nonsense verses. The army and the navy, too, laughed sardonically and musically at their monotonous food, their drudgery and the privileges of their officers.

Most of these songs had a flourishing existence long before they were committed to paper. Indeed, in the case of some of the occupational ones, it was only after the circumstances that had brought them forth had ceased to exist that the effort to preserve them was made. Varying versions of all of them have been printed and published.

13

In the later years of the nineteenth century it was the vaudeville shows which were the nuclei of song distribution. By 1900 song-writing was big business. A mounting stream of songs, a large portion of them humorous, issued from the booths of the publishers, were tried out by vaudeville teams and found their way in printed copies to millions of homes and pianos. The song business became centralized in New York, it gathered into a few offices in a few streets. It received a nickname: Tin Pan Alley.

Then came the phonographs. At first they encouraged the sale of sheet music. The scratchy sounds produced by them were a stimulation to, not a substitute, for home singing. But after 1922 came the radio with its fatally accurate reproduction of sound and speech. The best professional singing could be had at any time at the push of a button. The best song in the world could be worn to death in a few weeks. No song could build any affection with the public in such a feverish atmosphere of perpetual music palpitation. There are more songs now than there ever were, and just as good ones, but they don't seem to mean very much. We are compelled to love 'em and leave 'em every six weeks, are not allowed to keep steady company with any.

So it's no wonder that many people are turning to old songs. An old song is an old friend, nice and safe. It brings back memories of good times and pleasant feelings. It's a curious phenomenon: here we are, with some of our bang-up industrial machinery obsolete before it is put into production, looking for a little emotional security in the songs of generations ago.

It seems a particularly foolish and fruitless thing to do to try to analyze humor; it is a little like cutting open a drum to find out where the sound comes from. Part of humor's charm is its unreasonableness, its mystery. We will make no futile attempt at dissection, yet we will permit ourselves a few remarks which may possibly graze the surface of one or two facts of the truth.

It has been suggested, for instance, that humor is often the product of a sense of incongruity. That sounds true, as far as it goes. The improbable picture of "the monkey he got drunk, and climbed up the elephant's trunk" will get a laugh out of most people. So will the startling emotional juxtaposition of "de buckwheat cake war in her mouth, de tear war in her eye."

Intentional nonsense, the violent association of unrelated images, is also likely to arouse laughter as when

"Composed of sand was that favored land,

And trimmed with cinnamon straws;

And pink and blue with the pleasing hue

Of the tickle-tie toaster's claws."

Or the complete frustration of the faculty of language, as when the speech organs are used to fashion syllables devoid of denotation: "Co-ca-che-lunk che-lunk che-laly."

A favorite humorous type of incongruity is that between the extravagance of man's pretensions and the precariousness of their realization. Anyone will see the humor of the too eager swain who pursues the Gal with the Balmoral only to fall ignominiously on the ice; or of the foxy cowboys who try to discomfit the tenderfoot with Zebra Dun, the bad horse, only to find that the dude is a better rider than any of them. Or of the German struggling with the English language, or of the president of the fallen republic who supposedly has tried to escape capture dressed in his wife's hoopskirts.

15

It is, of course, fully realized that these examples are in themselves not *necessarily* humorous. A change of treatment, and the images they call forth might well be thought of as meaningless, absurd, or tragic, rather than laughable. Humor is where you find it—like gold, love and other good things. There is no guarantee that two different people will ever find it in the same place. Or, for that matter, that the same person will ever find it twice in the same place.

It might be hazarded that humor is, on the whole, an enemy of the extremes of dignity or self-importance. A sense of humor is a kind of sense of proportion, a sense of the reasonable limitations of individual human power. It is the little charge of explosive that bursts overinflated balloons and blasts down undue eminences. As such, humor is an expression of a peculiarly democratic frame of mind, and it seems natural that it should flourish with especial vigor in a land dedicated to the idea that no man is good enough to be another man's master.

There are other components of American humor. A good deal of it is hardly distinguishable from "good humor." There is perhaps nothing intrinsically funny about the idea of liking to eat meat, or about preparing the house for the visit of a relative. Yet the pictures of the Negro who is moved to music by his whole-hearted fondness for Good Ol' Sweet Ham, or of the New England family who fuss about busily and tunefully to make an impression on Cousin Jedediah, convey a feeling of lively well-being that will provoke a smile at any time, and a real laugh when set forth with verve and conviction.

Good humor, is, also, a true American quality. It rhymes with the inveterate optimism that has colored American life from the beginning. America has been a marvelous dream, even for those who have had it disturbed: In the history of the world America represents the

16

only opportunity the common man has ever had, on a grand scale, to advance his own well-being through his own efforts, untrammeled by traditional restrictions, and with a virgin continent of fabulous resources to work with.

A reckless enthusiasm for new projects, new gadgets, new leadership—an unquestioned belief in an unlimited progress, an uncontested conviction that despite any individual personal misfortunes, the world as a whole is getting better and better—all these have been, in the past, essential elements of the American mental atmosphere.

Humor and its relative, good humor, then, is a normal flavor of intercourse among democratic optimists, such as the Americans.

"Americans are the most musical people in the world."

A characteristically arrogant European intellectual, could he be induced to condescend to consider the above statement with any seriousness at all, would say: "You are making a pretty extravagant claim. Where are your Beethovens and your Toscanini's?"

The same European would have few skeptical qualms about the musicality of a country such as, say, Poland. Isn't there Chopin and isn't there Paderewski? The musical literacy of Poland's lower and middle classes, the number and quality of the orchestras it supports, the vitality and spread of its choral societies, the level of music education in its schools, the number of instruments it manufactures and purchases —all these your European intellectual will tend to disregard. Even the fact that neither Chopin nor Paderewski could make a living, let alone a career, in Poland will hardly impress him as important. Unreflectingly he thinks: "The country has two millionaires, (both living abroad) therefore the country is rich."

17

One cannot argue Europeans out of this point of view. It is a fundamental element of their mental make-up. Fifteen hundred years of feudalism and hierarchy have left a deeper groove in them than a paltry one hundred and fifty of liberalism. It is hard for them not to feel that only "great" men count, that the true humanity of the human race begins from the rank of baron on up, or from the degree of A.B., or, less assuredly, from the income of $10,000 a year. If anyone of humble origin, through sheer personal ability, makes a name for himself, they make him a baronet, give him an honorary degree and a pension just to make him seem complete.

Only in the last three or four generations have common people been shown on their stages, except to be laughed at, and the word "vulgar" is still a term of reproach.

Actually, music has been a part of America's essence ever since its beginnings. The first book of any kind to be published in English-speaking America, the "Bay Psalm Book," was a book of music, though it contained no notes. Music flourished in both Colonial New England and in the Colonial South. The Southern tradition is better known to us today. English and Irish rural ballads and ditties were sung by settlers and rovers from Virginia and Carolina on west; tunes and words were often modified to suit American conditions, but the songs have long since become genuine American. Their vigor is unabated. They are our oldest musical heritage.

After the Revolution there was a great upsurge of industrial and commercial enterprise in the cities. Foundations for a widespread middle-class prosperity were laid. The selling of sheet music became a plausible business. Numbers of music publishing firms sprang up in Philadelphia, Boston and Baltimore during the last decades of the

Eighteenth century. Many of them were established before some of the famous European publishers. As cities grew up further in the west their musical wants were in turn served by local publishers and dealers. There was a music publisher in Buffalo in 1828, in New Orleans in 1834. By the middle of the century they are found in Memphis, Mobile, Cleveland, St. Louis, Cincinnati, Louisville and San Francisco.

Entertainments of various kinds helped to intensify the general musical consciousness. Traveling troupes of singers popularized songs. So did minstrel shows, with their imitations of Negro musical habits. By the third quarter of the century single songs were boasting of sales of fifty thousand copies. The figure soon grew into the hundreds of thousands. During the first decades of the twentieth century, sales in the millions were common.

Closely allied to the spread of sheet music was the manufacture and distribution of pianos. According to one historian, the first piano was made in the United States as early as 1774. If that is true, it places American piano enterprise at the very base of piano history. It had been only five or six years since the first piano had ever been played in public in London. Pianos were imported and manufactured in increasing numbers throughout the early days of the Republic. By 1830 about four thousand pianos were sold annually in the United States.

American mechanical ingenuity began to exercise itself on the instrument. Several of its most outstanding improvements, such as the one-piece casting of the plate and the overstringing of the bass, were of American origin. All this was not merely a gratuitous ebullition of inventive lust: there was a dollar-sign behind these contraptions. Pianos were worth improving because there was a rapidly expanding

19

market for them; hundreds of thousands of people were anxious to buy them, play them, hear them.

At the International Exhibition at Paris in 1867, American pianos won numbers of the best awards, much to the astonishment of the Europeans. At that time our annual production had risen to about 30,000. By the turn of the century it was 100,000. By that time the piano was, like the garden hose and the rocking chair, an accepted middle-class American household god. Before its twilight in the 1920's it was being sold at the rate of 300,000 new units a year.

A steady stream of piano literature was proliferated to make fresh offerings to this domestic divinity. Songs were printed with piano accompaniments as a matter of course. Vast amounts of purely pianistic music were turned out. A dense spray of polkas, waltzes, marches, mazurkas, schottisches, redowas, quadrilles, two-steps, barn-dances, sentimental pieces, elegant "morceaux" and fancy variations whirred from the presses into innumerable front parlors. Furthermore a host of people, often whiskered foreigners and native old maids, were able to make livings teaching children and young ladies the gentle art of underpassing the thumb.

Intimately bound up with all this culture is the spread of musical literacy. It was in 1838 that Lowell Mason was able to introduce the study of music into the public schools of Boston on the ground that "through vocal music you set in motion a mighty power which silently, but surely, in the end, will humanize, refine and elevate a whole community." The refining influence upon the great masses—that was the reason given for teaching music to all the children in the schools, rather than only to those with outstanding special aptitude.

By 1846 Mason was already spreading his gospel as far west as

20

Cleveland, Ohio. By the end of the nineteenth century sight-singing was taught in the grade and high schools of a very large number of American cities, towns, and even villages. Tens of millions of people received systematic rudimentary musical instruction. In the larger centers the child without an opportuntity to learn to read notes was the exception rather than the rule.

During the twentieth century the public school music movement branched out vigorously in the instrumental field. By 1938 there were 30,000 high school orchestras throughout the land, some of them playing with astounding virtuosity, their members overwhelmingly innocent of any professional aspirations.

We need not go on with this pageant of American musicality. We need not speak of the development of church choirs, glee clubs, institutional choruses—of brass bands, theater and dance orchestras, etc. It is clear that the course of American history has proceeded to the accompaniment of a tremendous flow of self-made music.

"Oh, yes," says Herr von Hochnas, "you Americans have done a lot of yowling and doodling in your day—but look at it; it's all trash!"

One cannot dismiss the accusation lightly. It's pretty depressing to go through large collections of old American music. Great deserts of trite jingle spread out before one, sterile oceans of cheaply made, commonplace, cut-and-dried harmony, an endless, unrelieved repetition of the same infantile patterns. Ten thousand ballads, ditties, waltzes, all sliced with equal thinness off the same boloney. Vast repulsive swamps of sentimentality stretch through the old song volumes, giving off the nauseous aroma of sweethearts, mothers and children callously and mechanically killed in the second verse to squeeze tears and dimes from a soft-headed middle-class public.

21

However, one can say in defense of this music that it is entirely unpretentious. No single piece or song ever made a bid for any save the most short-lived attention. None of them was offered as drops of heart's blood from the bosoms of rare spirits. And yet, almost despite themselves, some of these modest productions have developed an astounding vitality. Apparently they are not all trash.

Today the operas of the "great" Meyerbeer and symphonies of the "great" Anton Rubinstein are mere epitaphs in the music encyclopedias; but many of Stephen Foster's nostalgic and humorous songs still arouse the affection of millions, after eighty years. Some of Sousa's marches are now seeing us cheerfully through their third war. Racy anonymous tunes such as the "Arkansas Traveller" and "The Turkey in the Straw" are more than a century old and still yielding elation.

Come to think of it, there are hundreds of songs and pieces like that. Come to think of it, America has a substantial body of permanent, potent musical lore.

One trouble is that disturbing word "art."

The European writers all call music an art. They assume it, they don't have to prove it, but the idea doesn't sit at all well with Joe Doakes. He has a distinct distaste for the word. "Art" to him suggests something elaborate and fussy and falsely mysterious, something fancy purchased by the rich and powerful to make them appear more magnificent, more aloof from the common man. Or again, "art" may suggest the reckless imaginings of an irresponsible eccentric, the wanton outpourings of a man so egoistical as not to seem to care whether anybody understands him or not. Or "art" may seem a kind of uselessly intricate hobby, a specialty of females and other idlers, to be tolerated

22

in good times, but hardly respected. Or "art" may seem a pedestal for exhibitions of personal snobbery on the part of unpleasant individuals educated beyond their intelligence.

In any case, "art" seems to picture something intensely unsociable.

"I wouldn't give five cents for all the art in the world," said Henry Ford. "You 'art' artists," former Mayor John F. Hylan flung contemptuously at a group of people who protested at a proposed disfigurement of Central Park. Walt Disney, they say, will not let the word "art" be used seriously in his studio.

The ordinary American has thought of music as an entertainment, as a muscular stimulant, as a sweetener of ceremonies and meetings, an expression of personal and communal exuberance, but not as an art. To take music, the most spontaneous of exercises, most direct of man's emotional essence, and turn it into an object of anxious analytical contemplation seems a perverse thing to do. To make music, most convival of activities, most powerful of binders between man and man, into a vehicle for social exclusiveness, or for personal conceit seems deliberately unkind, inhumane, cruel.

American music, then, is essentially popular music. Being popular makes it good. Music that is approved of becomes popular, and because it is popular it is approved. The song on everybody's lips, the tune that is the common experience of tens of millions of fellow Americans, usually is the good tune. Few Americans cherish the ambition to produce something rare and precious for a small coterie of connoisseurs. It is hard to sustain such a craving against the discouragements of an adverse moral climate.

American music is no different in its social aspect, from any

23

other American product. The genius of American production has always striven to supply the wants of the many rather than those of the few. In fact, such an attitude would seem to be a direct corollary of the democraitc way of life and thought. The inexpensive thing for millions of customers has been the ideal of American producers, not the exquisite plaything of dukes and millionaires. Much ingenuity has indeed been expanded on the improvement of American products, yet only with the underlying thought that they could be sold to vast masses of people.

The merchandise of the Seventh Avenue dress manufacturers is hardly worth a sneer to the haughty couturiers of the Rue de la Paix; it is in fact merely a corrupt and flimsy derivative of the latter's creations. Yet the former's goods selling at $6.98 and $12.75 are wonderful value for the money, and who would deny that American women, as a whole, are the best dressed women in the world? It is true that our Fords, Plymouths and Chevrolets cannot compare their points to the perfections of a Rolls-Royce. But we don't care much about making cars just for a few Morgan partners. And who would doubt that the American automobile, owned and driven by millions of the least of us, is in its way the most marvelous manufactured article ever brought forth by man?

Thus American popular music cannot be thought of in the same category as the creations of Wagner or Debussy. And yet, within the limits of its pretensions it is now an extraordinary article, full of resource and complexity and performed with outstanding skill; probably the most interesting popular music that has ever been evolved. Foreign countries have accepted it as such. American dance music and song tunes have spun triumphantly around the world; they have won decisive victories in the very citadels of the lands that brought Wagner and Debussy forth.

The present writer is quite aware that European concert and opera music has maintained a persistent and often spectacular career in this country. Historians of American music have been eager to point out, in defense of our "culture," that George Washington heard Haydn's symphonies at concerts, that "The Barber of Seville" had its first New York performance before it made its Paris debut, that the New York Philharmonic is older by a few years than the Vienna Philharmonic, that the Handel and Haydn Society of Boston was in correspondence with Beethoven, that the Boston Symphony Orchestra is acknowledged to be the finest in the world and that a hundred years' worth of brilliant, celebrated, and frequently supercilious, European musical executants have been able to stuff vast piles of unreluctant American dollars into their pockets as a result of their exhibitions.

All these activities have, until very recently, taken place among a small clique of foreign-minded people living in a few large cities. Either they are foreign-born or the immediate descendants of such, or they are the kind of Americans who are proud to know every dingy bar in Paris, every musty book-stall in London, but who have never troubled to gaze on Mount Shasta.

During the last twenty-five years, it is true, a great deal of European art music has thrust itself more widely and more deeply into our consciousness than ever before. Phonograph, radio and public school have contributed to the process. Quite a body of older European classics has been naturalized. Several hundred second and third class towns now have symphony orchestras, staffed by native Americans.

Concert music has lost its feeling of remoteness, of top-loftiness. Melodies by Mozart, Schubert, Chopin, Debussy and especially Tschaikowsky have been dished up, often rather gracelessly, as popular songs, but with due credit given.

But it is not certain whether all this activity has struck true roots in America. It resembles more an overlayer of decaying organic matter, incapable of further life in itself, but wonderful fertilizer for the viable seed germinating under it. America is looking forward to a flourishing musical future; but its maturer music will have to have the moral and financial support of millions, not mere thousands of people—it will have to speak a language not too far removed from the common American musical dialect as established by countless popular songs and dances. Furthermore, it will have to have its life in musical institutions developed by Americans for themselves, not in those, like the opera for instance, taken over from a hierarchical Europe.

This book will not escape the criticism that similar books have always had to suffer. Some people will complain that some things are included that they do not think worthwhile and that, on the other hand, a number of excellent things, perhaps their special favorites, have been omitted. There is no help for this state of affairs. Any practical book must be of reasonable size. In a compilation such as this, with a large amount of material to draw from, one has to stop somewhere. Now the point at which I wish to stop will of course not be the same point at which you would wish to stop. There seems little that can be done about these differences of taste. Let us hope the book contains enough stuff that both you and I like.

There is, however, one unavoidable shortcoming which may

well be pointed out in a book that aims to give a general survey of American popular songs. It is that it contains very few songs from our most prolific and interesting period of song composition, namely the years from about 1890-1925. All but a very few of these songs are still the private property of their publishers, who value them preciously; the cost of obtaining their various permissions to reprint any of them in complete form would be prohibitive. As the decades roll by, more and more of these songs will enter the public domain, and it may be hoped that our children will have the pleasure of pursuing collections that will enable them to relive the laughs of their grandfathers.

I wish to take this opportunity of expressing my deepest gratitude to Ruth Wilcox, head of the Fine Arts Division of the Cleveland Public Library, for the aid she has given me in preparing this book. Her interest in the subject as well as her knowledge and resourcefulness were of invaluable help.

My thanks are also due to Dr. Carleton Sprague Smith, chief of the Music Division of the New York Public Library, for his kindness in reading the preface and making some valuable suggestions.

ARTHUR LOESSER

Arranger's Note

IN MAKING THE PIANO ARRANGEMENTS FOR THIS volume I have been guided by the following principles: I have endeavored to make them so easy that the average amateur pianist will be able, for the most part, to play them at sight. Too thin or easy an accompaniment, however, might have robbed "The Regular Army" or "The Mulligan Guards" of their martial character.

Not many amateurs can read three staves simultaneously; therefore, with a few exceptions, the melody is included in the piano part.

I have tried to strike a happy medium between dullness and sophistication. A hackneyed accompaniment will scarcely be noticed if it is used in *one* song, but if used too often will ruin even the melodies of Foster. I have adhered to conventional chords where tradition seems well-established, but changed the customary setting where it is grammatically incorrect and unmusical. I have tried to fit the accompaniment to the style of the song: employed syncopation and "blue" chords in Negroid and minstrel songs, but avoided them in songs of English origin.

I have also attempted to preserve the modal feeling of the "Bird Song" and others.

ALFRED KUGEL

29

To FANNY ARMS
Recalling many gay musical evenings

Humor
in American Song

Sourwood Mountain

IN RECENT YEARS THE SOUTHERN MOUNTAIN
people have been the beneficiaries of rather intensive worship. The
Anglo-Saxon sector of our country has developed a kind of maudlin
crush on them. No doubt some vague ancestral nostalgia is at work here.

No other element of our population has received such affectionate attention. A vast library of fact and fiction has been written about them; serious treatises, fine novels, hack stories and trash. Mountain white people have been publicized, fictionized, idealized, romanticized, dramatized, lionized and generally fussed over and petted to a degree beyond any possible importance they have in the life of the nation. A wide and adoring audience is assured any real or make-believe hill-billy, from Sergeant York to Little Abner.

Apparently it is impossible to portray them unsympathetically. If they are poor it's wonderful, if they are dirty it's splendid, if they are illiterate it's marvelous, if they have trachoma it's superb, if they are bootleggers it's ravishing, if they commit incest it's glamorous, if they kill each other for pleasure it's rapturous, and if they kill strangers it's the seventy-seventh heaven of ecstacy.

Funny, though, how all these glories would turn to ashes if it were, say, Roumanians or Czechs one were talking about. But then, no group of Slav or Latin farmers however thrifty, well-schooled, healthy and law-abiding they were, could hope to completely overcome Anglo-Saxon distrust and prejudice. "Foreign" virtue could never be as interesting or attractive as English sin.

Amazing statements are made about the Southern mountain people. Again and again one or another of their apologists will make the astounding assertion that they are of "the finest stock." What a transparently naive way of saying that he loves them because they are English!

All this is somewhat irritating to those who, in the absence of any English ancestry, are incapable of viewing hill-billies with any but a fishy-eyed detachment. What they see is merely one more, and rather insignificant, group of backward people.

There are some indications of the twilight of the hill-billy. He has successfully run away from the school teacher and the doctor, and has bravely defied the tourist and the tax collector. Now he has been laid low by the musicologist. His weak spot has been breached. He has been unable to resist soft-spoken ladies and gentlemen who have asked for songs. They say he is now willing to sound his music off on a grand scale before large crowds of anonymous strangers. If he doesn't start in soon to shoot song collectors on sight with the same enthusiasm with which he used to pepper revenue officers, he and his progeny may look forward to a lifetime career as outdoor museum pieces.

Yet, the songs of these Southern mountain white folk probably are the oldest still extant American musical tradition. The uplands of the western part of Virginia and the Carolinas, the eastern part of Tennessee and Kentucky were settled, probably early in the eighteenth century, by people who had not long since come from England. The currents of American progress and development flowed around and past them and they lived for centuries in a rather tight isolation, self-encouraged if not self-imposed.

In the absence of strong outside influences, or of ambition, or imagination, the speech, customs, manners and songs of these people have remained pretty much the same for centuries. Most of their songs are substantially the same as they were when they brought them from England some two hundred years ago. The distinguished scholar, Cecil Sharp, made a profound study of these songs about twenty-five years ago, and he has named his collection "English Folksongs in the

Southern Appalachians." They are indeed English; apparently however, some of these songs have been modified in accordance with the American environment, and some few of them, it appears are of authentic American origin.

The songs are a normal accompaniment of various phases of these people's daily work and play. The imagery of the words is largely rural. Some of the songs are used for a type of youthful conviviality known as the "play-party." In this, gatherings of young people go through some patterned movements, groupings and pairings to tunes of their own singing—the whole thing, however, making a point of falling short of actual dancing.

On the musical side, it is interesting that the antiquity of some of these songs is indicated by the fact that they are sung in one or another of a number of ancient scale-modes antedating our major and minor. Some of them contain only five tones, as in the "Bird Song."

The native singers often accompany their songs on an instrument which they call a dulcimer. Apparently it differs from the instrument of that name as it has been known in parts of Europe. The European dulcimer-player strikes its strings with a hammer, the Americans pluck theirs.

Probably the favorite mountain instrument is the fiddle, played with or without singing. The tune given here, called "The Arkansas Traveller," is a genuine fiddle tune; if it is not directly from the Appalachians, it has much of the spirit of the music of that region. The conversation appended is, in its meaning, and even in the point of its jokes, the traditional concomitant of the melody. The actual sequence of the words has been taken from a treatise in the "Ohio Archeological Publications" by Thomas Wilson.

38

Bird Song

"Hi!" says the blackbird, sittin' on a chair,   "Once I court-ed a lad-y fair,

She proved fick - le and turned her   back,   And ever since

then,   I've dressed in   black."

2

"Hi!" says the woodpecker sittin' on a fence,
"Once I courted a handsome wench;
She proved fickle and from me fled—
And ever since then, my head's been red."

3

"Hi!" says the robin as away he flew,
"When I was a young man I chose two;
If one didn't love me, the other one would,
And don't you think my notion's good?"

Barnyard Song

1. Verse 1 goes from Section A directly to Section C.
2. Verse 2 goes from Section A through Section B once, then concludes with Section C.
3. All succeeding verses repeat Section B, adding all previous verses in reverse order. Conclusion is always with Section C.

2

I had a hen and the hen pleased me,
I fed my hen under yonder tree.
Hen goes chimmy-chuck, chimmy-chuck,
Cat goes fiddle-i-fee.

3

I had a duck and the duck pleased me,
I fed my duck under yonder tree.
Duck goes quack-quack,
Hen goes chimmy-chuck, chimmy-chuck,
Cat goes fiddle-i-fee.

4

I had a goose and the goose pleased me,
I fed my goose under yonder tree.
Goose goes swishy-swashy,
Duck goes quack-quack,
Hen goes chimmy-chuck, chimmy-chuck,
Cat goes fiddle-i-fee.

5

I had a sheep and the sheep pleased me,
I fed my sheep under yonder tree.
Sheep goes ba-ba,
Goose goes swishy-swashy,
Duck goes quack-quack,
Hen goes chimmy-chuck, chimmy-chuck,
Cat goes fiddle-i-fee.

6

I had a hog and the hog pleased me,
I fed my hog under yonder tree.
Hog goes griffy-gruffy,
Sheep goes ba-ba,
Goose goes swishy-swashy,
Duck goes quack-quack,
Hen goes chimmy-chuck, chimmy-chuck,
Cat goes fiddle-i-fee.

7

I had a cow and the cow pleased me,
I fed my cow under yonder tree,
Cow goes moo-moo,
Hog goes griffy-gruffy,
Sheep goes ba-ba,
Goose goes swishy-swashy,
Duck goes quack-quack,
Hen goes chimmy-chuck, chimmy-chuck,
Cat goes fiddle-i-fee.

8

I had a horse and the horse pleased me,
I fed my horse under yonder tree.
Horse goes neigh-neigh,
Cow goes moo-moo,
Hog goes griffy-gruffy,
Sheep goes ba-ba,
Goose goes swishy-swashy,
Duck goes quack-quack,
Hen goes chimmy-chuck, chimmy-chuck,
Cat goes fiddle-i-fee.

9

I had a dog and the dog pleased me,
I fed my dog under yonder tree.
Dog goes bow-wow,
Horse goes neigh-neigh,
Cow goes moo-moo,
Hog goes griffy-gruffy,
Sheep goes ba-ba,
Goose goes swishy-swashy,
Duck goes quack-quack,
Hen goes chimmy-chuck, chimmy-chuck,
Cat goes fiddle-i-fee.

Kissing Song

Fast

When a man falls in love with a little turtle dove, He will

linger all around her under jaw. He will kiss her for her mother and

sis-ter and broth'r Till her daddy comes and kicks him from the door. Draws a

pist-ol from his pock-et, pulls the ham-mer back to cock it, And vows

he'll blow a-way his gid-dy brains. Oh, his

ducky says he mustn't,'Tain't loaded and he doesn't, they're kissing one another once again.

From "Devil's Ditties" by Jean Thomas,
The Traipsin' Woman Founder of the
American Folk Song Festival.

2

The old maids love him, and the girls ain't above him,
Everybody's got a finger in the pie,
Some girls are just as haughty, and they say it's very naughty.
But you bet your life they kiss him on the sly;
When a girl is seventeen she thinks it very mean
If she cannot catch on something for a mash;
She'll pucker up her mouth, in a pretty little pout
And finger under his big mustache—

3

It will make a fellow shiver, he would like to jump the river.
They will stick as tight as granulated glue.
There is no use to tell her you're some other girl's fellow.
She will masticate your smeller if you do.
If you want to kiss her neatly, very sweetly, and completely
If you want to kiss her so as to kiss her nice
When you get a chance to kiss her, make a dodge or two and
        miss her.
Then sock her on the kisser once or twice.

Sourkraut

Not too fast

If you want to know how for to make the sour -
Chorus: Sourkraut is splen - did, sour - kraut is

kraut, Just o - pen up your ears and I'll tell you all a -
fine, We thinks we ought to know him, for we eats him all the

bout, It is - n't made of leath - er as man - y sup -
time, Sour - kraut is splen - did, sour - kraut is

pose, It's made of the good old flow - er we call the cabbage rose.
fine, We thinks we ought to know him, for we eats him all the time.

From "Devil's Ditties" by Jean Thomas,
The Traipsin' Woman Founder of the
American Folk Song Festival.

When this flower grows up just as big as he can be,
We cuts him in small pieces, no bigger'n a pea,
We puts him in the barrel, where he begins to smell
S'help me goodness gracious, don't this Dutchman love him well!

3

Puts in some cayenne pepper, we don't put any snuff,
We puts a little salt and some other kind of stuff.
Puts him in a barrel and when he begins to smell
S'help me goodness gracious, don't this Dutchman love him well!

When this kraut begins to smell till he can't get any smeller,
Puts him in a barrel and takes him down the cellar,
Puts him in a kittle and when he begins to bile
Bet you forty dollars you can smell him fifty mile.

Frog Went A-Courting

Frog went a-court-ing and he did ride

Rink-tum bod-y min-chy cam-bo Sword and buck-ler

by his side Rink-tum bod-min-chy cam-bo.

Chorus:

Ki-ma-nee-ro down to Cai-ro Ki-ma-nee-ro

Cai - ro Strad - dle - ad - dle lad - da - bob - bo

Lad - da - bob - bo link - tum Rink - tum bod - y min - chy

cam - bo.

2

He rode down by the mill side door
Rinktum body minchy cambo
To hear his saddle squeak and roar
Rinktum body minchy cambo.

3

He rode down to Lady Mouse's house
Rinktum body minchy cambo
The old mouse was not at home.
Rinktum body minchy cambo.

4

The old mouse came home at last
Rinktum body minchy cambo
Shook her big fat sides and laughed.
Rinktum body minchy cambo.

5

He took Miss Mousie on his knee
Rinktum body minchy cambo
Pray Miss Mousie will you marry me?
Rinktum body minchy cambo.

6

Who will make the wedding gown?
Rinktum body minchy cambo
Old Miss Rat from pumpkin town.
Rinktum body minchy cambo.

7

Where will the wedding breakfast be?
Rinktum body minchy cambo
Way down yonder in a hollow tree.
Rinktum body minchy cambo.

8

What will the wedding supper be?
Rinktum body minchy cambo
A fried mosquito and a roasted flea.
Rinktum body minchy cambo.

9

First came in was a bumble bee
Rinktum body minchy cambo
A fiddle buckled on his knee
Rinktum body minchy cambo.

10

Next came in were two little ants
Rinktum body minchy cambo
Fixing around to have a dance.
Rinktum body minchy cambo.

11

Next came in was a little flea
Rinktum body minchy cambo
To dance a jig for the bumble bee.
Rinktum body minchy cambo.

12

Next came in was a big black snake
Rinktum body minchy cambo
Passing round the wedding cake.
Rinktum body minchy cambo.

13

Next came in was a big black bug
Rinktum body minchy cambo
On his back was a whiskey jug.
Rinktum body minchy cambo.

14

Next came in was a big Tom cat
Rinktum body minchy cambo
Swallowed up mouse and growled at the rat.
Rinktum body minchy cambo.

15

Frog jumped up and winked his eye
Rinktum body minchy cambo
Wished to hell the cat would die.
Rinktum body minchy cambo.

Sourwood Mountain

Fast

My true love lives over the moun-tain, Hey ding did – dle,
did – dle dad – dy day. I would give this world if I was with her,
Hey ding did – dle dad – dy day.

2

I got a girl at the head of the holler,
Hey ding diddle, diddle daddy day.
She won't come and I won't foller,
Hey ding diddle-daddy day.

3

Say, old man, I want your daughter,
Hey ding diddle, diddle daddy day.
To wash my clothes and carry my water,
Hey ding diddle-daddy day.

4

Big dog barks and little one'll bite you,
Hey ding diddle, diddle daddy day.
Big gal court an' little one'll marry you,
Hey ding diddle-daddy day.

5

Ducks in the pond and geese in the ocean,
Hey ding diddle, diddle daddy day.
Devil's in the women if they take a notion,
Hey ding diddle-daddy day.

Old Joe Clark

2

Old Joe's got an old red cow,
I know her by the bell;
If she ever gets in my cornfield
I'll shoot her shore as hell.

3

Old Joe had a yellow cat,
She would not sing or pray,
Stuck her head in a buttermilk jar
And washed her sins away.

4

I went up to Old Joe's house,
Old Joe wasn't at home;
I ate up all his ham meat
And throwed away the bone.

Chorus:

Round and round all Old Joe Clark,
Round and round I say;
He'll foller me ten thousand miles
To hear my fiddle play.

5

I won't go down to Old Joe's house,
I told you that before;
He fed me in a hog trough,
And I won't go there any more.

6

I went up to Old Joe's house,
Old Joe wasn't at home;
Jumped in bed with Old Joe's wife
And broke her tucking comb.

7

I wish I was in Tennessee
Sittin' in a big armchair,
One arm round a whisky jug,
Other one round my dear.

8

I climbed up on the old oak tree,
And she climbed up the gum;
I never saw a pretty girl
But what I loved her some.

9

When I was a little girl
I used to play with toys;
Now I am a bigger girl
I'd rather play with boys.

10

When I was a little boy
I used to want a knife;
But now I am a bigger boy
All I want is a wife.

11

Wish I was a sugar tree
Standin' in the middle of some town;
Every time a pretty girl passed
I'd shake some sugar down.

The Arkansas Traveller

TRAVELLER: How do you do, stranger?

SQUATTER: Do pretty much as I please, sir. (Plays first part.)

TRAVELLER: Stranger, do you live about here?

SQUATTER: I reckon I don't live anywheres else! (Plays first part only.)

TRAVELLER: Well, how long have you lived here?

SQUATTER: See that big tree there? Well, that was there when I come. (Plays first part.)

TRAVELLER: Well, you don't need to be so cross about it; I wasn't asking no improper questions at all!

SQUATTER: I reckon there's nobody cross here except yourself! (Plays first part only.)

TRAVELLER: How did your potatoes turn out here last year?

SQUATTER: They didn't turn out at all; we dug 'em out. (Plays first part only.)

TRAVELLER: Can I stay here all night?

SQUATTER: Yes, you kin stay right where you air, out en the road. (Plays first part.)

TRAVELLER: How far is it to the next tavern?

SQUATTER: I reckon it's upwards of some distance. (Plays first part.)

TRAVELLER: How long will it take to get there?

SQUATTER: You'll not git there at all, if ye stay here foolin' with me. (Plays first part.)

TRAVELLER: How far is it to the forks of the road?

SQUATTER: It ain't forked since I been here. (Plays.)

TRAVELLER: Where does this road go to?

SQUATTER: It ain't gone anywhere since I been here—jist stayed right here. (Plays.)

TRAVELLER: Why don't you put a new roof on your house?

SQUATTER: Because it's rainin' and I can't. (Plays.)

TRAVELLER: Why don't you do it when it is not raining?

SQUATTER: It don't leak then. (Plays.)

TRAVELLER: Can I get across the branch down here?

SQUATTER: I reckon you kin, the ducks cross whenever they want to. (Plays.)

TRAVELLER: Why don't you play the rest of the tune?
(The player stops as quick as lightning.)

SQUATTER: Gee, stranger, can you play the rest of that tune? I've been down to New Orleans and I heard it at the theatre, and I've been at work at it ever since I got back, trying to get the last part of it. If you can play the rest of that tune, you kin stay in this cabin for the rest of your natural life. Git right down, hitch your horse and come in! I don't keer if it is a-rainin'! I don't keer if the beds is all full! We'll make a shake-down on the floor and ye kin kiver with the door. We hain't got much to eat, but what we have, you're mighty welcome to it. Here, Sal, old woman, fly round and git some corndodgers and bacon for the gentleman—he knows the last part of the tune! Don't you, stranger—didn't you say you did? . . . If you know it, you are a friend and a 'brother-come-to-me-arms'; if you don't, you've excited the tiger in my bosom and I'll have nothing short of your heart's blood! Git down, git down!

TRAVELLER: Yes, I can play it; there's no use of your getting mad. I'll play it for you as soon's I get something to eat.

SQUATTER: Fly 'round here; old woman, set the table, bring out the knives and forks.

(Here the little boy has to put in his oar and say: "Daddy, you know we haven't got any forks, and there ain't any knives to go 'round.")

SQUATTER: Like to know why there ain't! There's little butch and big butch, and whort handle and cob handle, and no handle at all, and if that ain't knives enough to set any gentleman's table in this country, I would like to know! Git off'n your hoss, stranger, and come in and have some-th'n, and then play the rest of that tune.

Liza Jane

2

I ask little Liza to marry me; what do you reckon she said?
She said she would not marry me if everybody else were dead.

3

I wish I was an apple a-hangin' on the tree
And ev'ry time my true love passed, she'd take a bite of me.

4

Wish I had a needle and thread as fine as I could sew,
I would sew my true love to my side and down the river I'd go.

5

I'll go up on the mountain top, and plant me a patch of cane;
I'll make me a jug of molasses, for to sweeten Liza Jane.

6

Went to see my Liza Jane, she was standin' in the door,
Shoes and stockin's in her hand, and her feet all over the floor.

7

Head is like a coffee-pot, nose is like a spout;
Her mother is like an old fire-place, with the ashes all raked out.

8

Th' hardest work I ever did was a-brakin' on the train;
Easiest work that I ever did was huggin' Liza Jane.

9

Whisky by the barrel, sugar by the pound;
A great big bowl to put it in, and a spoon to stir it round.

Cumberland Gap

Gaily

Me an' my wife' an' my wife's gran'-pap

All raise hell in Cum-ber-land Gap.

Piano

2
The first white man in Cumberland Gap
Was Doctor Walker, an English chap.

3
Daniel Boone on Pinnacle Rock
He killed Indians with his old flintlock.

4
I've got a woman in Cumberland Gap,
She's got a boy that calls me Pap.

5
Lay down boys and take a little nap,
They're raisin' hell in Cumberland Gap.

Blue Tory Noses

S.M.Adler

HERE ARE A FEW SONGS DIRECTLY BEARING ON THE
crisis that gave the nation birth. They have touches of humor and
are worth preserving for sentimental and historical reasons. The tunes,
with one conceivable exception, are all of English origin. This was

hardly an obstacle to their becoming a vehicle for robustly anti-British feeling.

" 'Twas Winter and Blue Tory Noses" is a parody on an English song called "The Banks of the Dee." The latter was originally written by John Trait. It is the lament of a girl whose lover has gone off to put down the "rebels." The American words were composed by Oliver Arnold, a relative of the inglorious traitor. He was inspired to this effort during 1775, when early conflicts were already taking place.

"What a Court Hath Old England" was also written in 1775, when hostilities had opened, but independence had not yet been proclaimed, though many people had it in mind. The tune was a popular English song called "Derry, Down Derry." According to Mr. J. Tasker Howard, the words "Goody Bull and Her Daughter" may well have been sung to the same melody previously. These words date from 1767, after the irksome tax acts had been passed by Parliament, but when reconciliation was still a reasonable possibility.

"The Battle of the Kegs" relates an actual incident of the war. During the British occupation of Philadelphia an inventive American had the bright idea of floating some kegs. filled with about one hundred and fifty pounds of powder, down the Delaware river so that they would explode on contact with British ships. The bombs were badly timed, most of the kegs went off on the ice although one ship, it is said, was damaged. But the British soldiers grew panicky when they saw and heard the explosions, and fired pell mell into the river. Ships sent out broadsides, bullets poured out from the decks. General Howe, Commander of the British forces, was awakened despite the reported fact that he was busily engaged for the night. The ludicrousness of the entire situation appealed to Francis Hopkinson, and he penned the satirical

62

verses. The tune is "Yankee Doodle," already very popular at the time.

Francis Hopkinson was a lawyer, a gentleman of distinction, and not least, a musician of considerable ability. He is generally regarded as one of the very earliest literate American composers.

"How Happy the Soldier" was very popular with the British army during the Revolution. Apparently the Americans enjoyed it no less, for it appears in the "American Musical Miscellany," published at Northampton in 1798. A purely American version of the words is said to have appeared during the War of 1812.

We will prefer to offend the intelligence of some readers, rather than have any of them missing the point in the first verse, by informing them that "half-a-crown" is about sixty-two cents in gold, while "six-pence" is little more than a lowly dime.

It is interesting to observe that all except one of these songs is in 6/8 meter. The English have always had a peculiar fondness for this jiggy rhythm; it has hopped through their songs for a long, long time. We find it in "Sumer is icumen in" as far back as 1230, we hear it in "Lilybulero" in the seventeenth century, in "Pop Goes the Weasel" in the eighteenth; and Sulivan was in the best English tradition when he used it in "She's Going to Marry Yum-Yum Today," and many other songs.

What a Court Hath Old England

Spiritedly

What a court hath old Eng-land, of fol-ly and sin, Spite of

Chath-am Cam-den, Barre, Burke, Wilks and Glynn! Not con-

tent with the game act, they tax fish and sea, And Am-

er-i-ca drench with hot wat-er and tea Der-

down, down, hey der-ry down.

2

There's no knowing where this oppression will stop,
Some say there's no cure but a capital chop;
And that I believe's each American's wish,
Since you've drenched them with tea and deprived them of fish.
    Derry down, down, hey derry down.

3

Three generals these mandates have borne 'cross the sea,
To deprive them of fish and to make 'em drink tea;
In turn, sure, these freemen will boldly agree
To give 'em a dance upon Liberty Tree.
    Derry down, down, hey derry down.

4

And *freedom's* the word, both at home and abroad,
And damn every scabbard that hides a good sword;
Our forefathers gave us this freedom in hand,
And we'll die in defence of the rights of the land.
    Derry down, down, hey derry down.

Goody Bull
To the tune of "What a Court Hath Old England"

1

Goody Bull and her daughter together fell out
Both squabbled and wrangled and made a damned rout,
But the cause of the quarrel remains to be told,
Then lend both your ears an da tale I'll unfold.

2

The old lady it seems took a freck in her head
That her daughter, grown woman, might earn her own bread.
Self-applauding her scheme, she was ready to dance;
But we're often too sanguine in what we advance.

3

In vain did the matron hold forth in the cause,
That the young one was able, her duty, the laws;
Ingratitude vile, disobedience far worse;
But she might e'en as well sung psalms to a horse.

4

Young, forward and sullen, and vain of her beauty,
She tartly replied, that she knew well her duty,
That other folks' children were kept by their friends,
And that some folks loved people but for their own ends.

5

Alas! cried the old woman and must I comply?
But I'd rather submit than the hussy should die;
Pooh, prithee, be quiet, be friends and agree
You must surely be right, *if you're guided by me.*

The Battle of the Kegs

2

As, in amaze, he stood to gaze;
The truth can't be denied, sirs,
He spied a score—of kegs—or more,
Come floating down the tide, sirs.
A sailor, too, in jerkin blue,
The strange appearance viewing,
First damned his eyes in great surprise,
 Then said, "Some mischief brewing."

3

"The kegs now hold the rebel bold
Packed up like pickled herring;
And they've come down to attack the town
In this new way of ferrying."
The soldier flew, the sailor, too,
And, scared almost to death, sirs,
Wore out their shoes to spread the news,
And ran till out of breath, sirs.

4

Now up and down, throughout the town,
Most frantic scenes were acted;
And some ran here and some ran there,
Like men almost distracted.
Some "fire" cried, which some denied,
But said the earth had quakéd;
And girls and boys, with hideous noise,
Ran through the town half-naked.

5

Sir William, he, snug as a flea,
Lay all this time a-snoring,
Nor dreamed of harm, as he lay warm
In bed with ———
Now, in a fright, he starts upright,
Awakened by such a clatter;
He rubs both eyes and boldly cries,
"For God's sake, what's the matter?"

6

At his bedside he then espied
Sir Erskine at command, sirs;
Upon one foot he had a boot,
And t'other in his hand, sirs.
"Arise! Arise!" Sir Erskine cries;
"The rebels—more's the pity—
Without a boat are all afloat,
 And ranged before the city."

7

"The motley crew, in vessels new
With Satan for their guide, sir,
Packed up in bags, or wooden kegs,
Come driving down the tide, sir.
Therefore, prepare for bloody war!
Those kegs must all be routed,
Or surely we despised shall be,
And British courage doubted."

8

The royal band now ready stand,
All ranged in dead array, sirs,
With stomach stout to see it out,
And make a bloody day, sirs.
The cannons roar from shore to shore,
The small arms make a rattle;
Since wars began, I'm sure no man
E'er saw so strange a battle.

9

The rebel vales, the rebel dales,
With rebel trees surrounded,
The distant woods, the hills and floods,
With rebel echoes sounded.
The fish below swam to and fro,
Attacked from every quarter—
"Why, sure," thought they, "the devil's to pay
'Mongst folks above the water."

10

The kegs, 'tis said, tho' strongly made
Of rebel staves and hoops, sirs,
Could not oppose the powerful foes,
The conquering British troops, sirs.
From morn to night these men of might
Displayed amazing courage,
And when the sun was fairly down
Returned to sup their porridge.

11

A hundred men, with each a pen,
Or more—upon my words, sirs,
It is most true—would be too few
Their valor to record, sirs,
Such feats did they perform that day
Upon those wicked kegs, sirs,
That years to come, if they get home,
They'll make their boasts and brags, sirs.

How Happy the Soldier

Slow march time

How hap – py the sol – dier who lives on his pay, And spends half a crown on six – pence a day; He fears neith – er just – ic – es' war – rants or bums But pays all his debts with a roll of his drums, With a row de dow, row de dow, row de dow, dow, And he

pays all his debts with a roll of his drums.

2

He cares not a marnedy how the world goes,
His King finds his quarters and money and clothes;
He laughs at all sorrow whenever it comes,
And rattles away with a roll of his drums,
With a row de dow, row de dow, row de dow, dow,
And he pays all his debts with a roll of his drums.

3

The drum is his glory, his joy and delight,
It leads him to pleasures as well as to fight;
No girl when she hears it though ever so glum,
But packs up her tatters and follows the drum.
With a row de dow, row de dow, row de dow, dow,
And he pays all his debts with a roll of his drums.

'Twas Winter and Blue Tory Noses

Vigorously (Parody on The Banks of the Dee)

'Twas win - ter and blue Tor-y nos – es were freezing As they marched o'er the land where they ought not to be; The val – iants com – plained at the fif – ers' cursed wheez-ing And wished they'd re – mained on the banks of the Dee. Lead on, thou paid cap - tain! Tramp on, thou proud min - ions! Thy

ranks, bas - est men, shall be strung like ripe on - ions, For
here thou hast found heads with war - like op - in - ions On
shoul - ders of no - bles who ne'er saw the Dee.

2

Prepare for war's conflict, or make preparation
For peace with the rebels, for they're brave and glee;
Keep mindful of dying and keep the foul nation
That sends out its armies to brag and to flee.
Make haste now, and leave us, thou miscreant Tories!
To Scotland repair! There court the sad houris,
And listen once more to their plaints and their stories
Concerning the "glory and pride of the Dee."

3

Be quiet and sober, secure and contented:
Upon your own land be valiant and free;
Bless God that the war is so nicely prevented
And till the green fields on the banks of the Dee.
The Dee will then flow, all its beauty displaying,
The lads on its banks will again be seen playing
And England thus honestly taxes defraying
With natural drafts from the banks of the Dee.

Apron Strings

ONE'S FEELING OF INFERIORITY IS NOT NECESSARI-
ly based on a reasoned conviction. It may merely be the unconscious
acceptance of the valuation of others. If enough people tell you that
you look ill, you will feel there must be something to it, even though

your mirror will not confirm the fact. Children uncritically accept the notion of their dependence from their parents; they can't help getting it, since it's a notion always floating around at home. The point is, they still feel it even after they know it isn't true.

The Americans must have been in some such state of mind during the first sixty years after the Declaration of Independence. For a century and a half the Americans had known themselves to be colonials; they accepted British ideas as unquestioningly as they accepted British manufactured products. Indeed, there were hardly any other ideas for them to get. And among these ideas was the assumption of their own status of inferiority.

Later, conflicting interests developed, and the glories of Bunker Hill, Valley Forge and Yorktown were achieved. The United States were organized, the Americans now had a proud government of their own, with all appurtenances: coinage, courts, a flag. But the habits of nearly a hundred and fifty years of tutelage could hardly be wiped out by a pen-stroke on a treaty. Any boy celebrating his twenty-first birthday could understand that. For a long time British products, material and spiritual, poured into the country. English books, plays and music were the normal fare for most literate Americans.

At the same time it was a great age of national pride, enterprise and expansion. Boastful spread-eagle slogans filled the air, many of them directed against the British: "We have met the enemy and they are ours"; Millions for defense, but not one cent for tribute"; "Columbia, the Gem of the Ocean." General Andrew Jackson defeated the British in a futile battle at New Orleans, months after a treaty of peace had been signed, and its ineffectual glory netted him an undying popularity, and eventually the Presidency.

It was at about the time of his election that a genuine American cultural independence was beginning to be thought of. That was when Noah Webster first published his famous dictionary, in which he boldly changed the time-honored spelling of many common English words, and when it was even suggested that the language of the country be called "Statish" instead of English. Here it was the speech of the less-lettered common man that was of deciding moment, the man whose habits were not dominated by the influence of imported print.

Music lagged in this movement. Americans began to write texts of songs, but the largest proportion of them were supposed to be sung to already existing tunes, mostly from England. In fact, the music seemed to be regarded as a secondary phase of the song. Either for that reason, or because few people could read notes, however literate they might, be most of the old collections of songs called "songsters" contained no music.

When Francis Scott Key wrote his immortal ode to the star-spangled banner, he could think of nothing better than to fashion it to the tune of an English drinking song, which had already been used once before to mother some American patriotic verses. As early as 1816, James Hewitt tried to remedy the situation and composed his own music to the celebrated words, but nobody paid much attention; and Hewitt was British born at that.

There is some evidence that "Columbia, the Gem of the Ocean" is a mere return-ticket of a previous "Britannia, the Gem of the Ocean." And it seems a little strange now that when the Reverend Dr. Smith, early in the 1830's started every school child stating his devotion to the "sweet land of liberty," he should have sewed it fast to the tones traditionally used to express deathless loyalty to the gracious, glorious, victorious king of England.

Of course, native American tunes did come forth, little by little. Still, as late as 1845 a collection called the "Virginia Warbler" says: "In this selection it was thought best to include a liberal share of the strains of our native bards, who, to say the least, do not fall *much* below their transatlantic contemporaries." Pretty timid talk for people who were yelling, "Fifty-four forty or fight!" and "On to Mexico." It was only after 1850, when the minstrel troupes became universally popular, that purely native songs dominated the scene.

Of the songs given here, "Nothing like Grog," "Nobody" and "Tom Tackle" are quite English in feeling, speech and atmosphere. The first two have a peculiar British ribaldry, which still manages to remain grammatical. It makes one think of regency rakes. The songs are older than that, however, having been found in the "American Musical Miscellany" of 1798.

"Amo, Amas," came from a ballad opera by Dr. Samuel Arnold, much-enjoyed English composer of light music during the late eighteenth century. Its hog-Latin would be amusing to an age in which Latin was still thought to be the basis of all learning and the badge of the gentleman. Miss Ruth Wilcox, of Cleveland, says that there is a tradition in her family to the effect that her great-great-grandfather sang the song when he was a student at Dartmouth College not long after the Revolution. So we may claim it as naturalized.

The songs "Analization," "The Tea Tax," "Tongo Island" and "Chit Chat" date from the 1830's. They have all the marks of having been first promulgated from the stage, where the singer's voice, gesture, costume and manner would all enhance their effect. By the way, the

76

spelling of "Analization" is that of the original. Its verses about various towns such as Baltimore, New York, etc. were probably rarely sung at any one rendition. The performer no doubt reserved each one for the particular city in which he happened to be putting on his act, thus making the audience feel important, an old stage trick.

"The Tea Tax" is undoubtedly a purely native song. It evinces a rather blatant sort of Americanism, emphasizing a rather self-conscious Yankee type. George Stuyvesant Jackson, in his book, "The Early Songs of Uncle Sam," described it thus: "Any character who said 'snum,' 'tarnal,' or 'plaguy' was a true blue Yankee, a rough diamond but worth his weight in gold and able to lick his weight in wild cats, thus becoming thoroughly commonplace."

The Boston Tea Party, by the time of this song, had passed into history more than sixty years before, and in any event was not a world-shaking occurrence. But people never seemed to tire of hearing about it. It gave them more real satisfaction than the battle of Saratoga or the treaty of Paris. And why not? It was a masquerade, a surprise party, there was lots of fun busting things, John Bull got a kick in the pants and nobody got really hurt.

In "Chit Chat" perhaps we ought to explain that a "reticule" is a woman's net bag, and that "cheapen" is an obsolete word meaning to shop or bargain.

The "Sir Humphry" who is mentioned in the introduction to "Analization" is probably Sir Humphry Davy, famous British chemist, discoverer of "laughing gas."

Nothing Like Grog

2

My father, when last I from Guinea
    Return'd with abundance of wealth,
Cried—Jack, never be such a ninny
    To drink—Says I—father, your health.
So I pass'd round the stuff—soon he twigg'd it,
    And it set the old codger agog,
        And he swigg'd, and mother,
        And sister and brother,
And I swigg'd, and all of us swigg'd it,
    And swore there was nothing like grog.

3

One day, when the Chaplain was preaching,
    Behind him I curiously slunk,
And, while he our duty was teaching,
    As how we should never get drunk,
I tipt him the stuff, and he twigg'd it,
    Which soon set his rev'rence agog.
        And he swigg'd, and Nick swigg'd,
        And Ben swigg'd, and Dick swigg'd,
    And I swigg'd, and all of us swigg'd it,
        And swore there was nothing like grog.

4

Then trust me, there's nothing as drinking
    So pleasant on this side the grave;
It keeps the unhappy from thinking,
    And makes e'en more valiant the brave.
For, me, from the moment I twigg'd it,
    The good stuff has so set me agog,
        Sick or well, late or early,
        Wind foully or fairly,
    I've constantly swigg'd it,
        And dam' me there's nothing like grog.

Chit Chat

Neatly, lightly, prettily, with lots of staccato

By P. K. Moran

Pret - ty lit - tle dam - sels, how they chat,

Chit, chat, tit - tle tat - tle tat.

All a - bout their sweet - hearts and all that

Chit, chat, tit - tle tat - tle tat.

2

Pretty little damsels go to cheapen in the shops,
Chit, chat, tittle tattle tat.
Pretty little bonnet and pretty little caps, and
Chit, chat, tittle tattle tat.
A little bit of rouge and a pretty little fan,
A pretty little miniature of a pretty little man,
On any other pretty little thing of which they can
Chit, chat, tittle tattle tat.

3

Pretty little damsels go to feast their eyes—
Chit, chat, tittle tattle tat.
But the splendid panorama cannot suffice,
Chit, chat, tittle tattle tat.
Their pretty parasols to keep their faces cool,
And their pretty little veils under which they play the fool
And upon their pretty arm the pretty reticule all for
Chit, chat, tittle tattle tat.

4

Pretty little damsels, how prettily they run,
Chit, chat, tittle tattle tat.
For a bit of flattery and a little bit of fun,
Chit, chat, tittle tattle tat.
The pretty little nose and the pretty little chin
The pretty little mouth with a pretty little grin,
The pretty little tongue to keep admirers in
Chit, chat, tittle tattle tat.

5

Pretty little damsels when they're wed,
Hum, dum, diddle diddle dum.
Their pretty little foibles are all fled
Hum, dum, diddle diddle dum.
Their pretty little airs so bewitchingly wild
Evaporate so prettily and leave them so mild
Then all their tittle-tattle's about the little child,
Hum, dum, diddle diddle dum.

Amo, Amas

Moderato

Words by O'Keefe

A - mo, a - mas, I love a

lass As a ced - ar tall and slen -

der. Sweet cow - slip's grace is her nom - in- at - ive

case And she s of the fem- in -ine gen - der.

Refrain:

Ro - rum, co - rum, sunt di - vo - rum

84

Ha - rum sca - rum di - vo;

Tag - rag, mer - ry - der - ry, per - i - wig and hat - band,

Hic hoc ho - rum gen - it - i - vo.

2

Can I decline a Nymph divine—
Her voice as a flute is dulcis;
Her oculus bright, her manus white,
And soft, when I tacto, her pulse is.

3

Oh, how bella, my puella,
I'll kiss her secula seculorum;
If I've luck, sir, she's my uxor,
O dies benedictorum!

Tom Tackle

Tom Tack - le was nob - le, was true to his
word, If mer - it bought tit - les, Tom might be my
lord: How gay - ly his bark thro' life's o - cean would
fail, Truth fur - nish'd the rig - ging, and hon - our the
gale: Yet Tom had a fail - ing if

know what this fault was, Tom Tack-le was

poor, Tom Tack-le was poor, Tom Tack-le was

poor, Tom Tack-le was poor. Wou'd you

know what this fault was, Tom Tack-le was poor.

2

'Twas once on a time, when we took a galleon,
And the crew touch'd the agent for cash to some tune;
Tom a trip took to prison, an old messmate to free,
And four thankful prattlers soon sat on each knee:
Then Tom was an angel, downright from heav'n sent,
While they'd hands, he his goodness should never repent,
Return'd from next voyage, he bemoan'd his hard case,
To find his dear friend, shut the door in his face
Why d'ye wonder, cried one, you're serv'd right to be sure,
Once Tom Tackle was rich, now Tom Tackle is poor.

3

I be'nt, you see, vers'd in high maxims and sich,
But don't this same honour concern poor and rich,
If it don't come from good hearts, I can't see where from,
And damme is e'er tar had good heart 't was Tom:
Yet somehow or other, Tom never did right,
None knew better the time when to spare or to fight:
He by finding a leak, once preserv'd crew and ship,
Sav'd the commodore's life— Then he made such rare slip,
And yet for all this, no one Tom cou'd endure,
I fancy as how 't was because he was poor.

4

At last an old shipmate that Tom might hail land,
Who saw that his heart fail'd too fast for his hand,
In the riding of comfort, a mooring to find,
Reef'd the sails of Tom's fortune, that shook in the wind;
He gave him enough thro' life's ocean to steer,
Be the breeze what it may, steady, thus or too near.
His pittance is daily, and yet Tom imparts,
What he can to his friends.—And may all honest hearts,
Like Tom Tackle, have what keeps the wolf from the door,
Just enough to be gen'rous, too much to be poor—

Nobody

If to force me to sing it be your in-ten-tion, Some-
one I will hint at, yet no-bod-y men-tion, No-
bod-y you'll cry, pshaw, that must be stuff, At
sing-ing I'm no-bod-y, that's the first proof,
No, no-bod-y, no, no-bod-y,

no - bod - y,   no - bod - y,   no - bod - y,   no.

2

Nobody's a name everybody will own,
When something they ought to be asham'd to have done;
'Tis a name well applied to old maids and young beaus,
What they were intended for nobody knows.
    No, nobody, no, nobody, nobody, nobody, nobody, no.

3

If negligent servants should china-plate crack,
The fault is still laid on poor nobody's back;
If accidents happen at home or abroad,
When nobody's blam'd for it, is not that odd?
    No, nobody, no, nobody, nobody, nobody, nobody, no.

4

Nobody can tell you the tricks that are play'd,
When nobody's by, betwixt master and maid!
She gently crys out, "Sir, there'll somebody hear us."
He softly replies, "My dear, nobody's near us."
    No, nobody, no, nobody, nobody, nobody, nobody, no.

5

But big with child proving, she's quickly discarded,
When favors are granted, nobody's rewarded;
And when she's examined, crys, "Mortals, forbid it,
If I'm got with child, it was nobody did it."
    No, nobody, no, nobody, nobody, nobody, nobody, no.

6

When by stealth, the gallant, the wanton wife leaves,
The husband's affrighten'd, and thinks it is thieves;
He rouses himself, and crys loudly, "Who's there?"
The wife pats his cheek, and says, "Nobody, dear."
    No, nobody, no, nobody, nobody, nobody, nobody, no.

7

Enough now of nobody sure has been sung,
Since nobody's mention'd, nor nobody's wrong'd;
I hope for free speaking I may not be blam'd,
Since nobody's injured, nor nobody's nam'd.
    No, nobody, no, nobody, nobody, nobody, nobody, no.

Tongo Island

Dedicated to the Princess Waskey Taw

By T. W. Moncrief

We got thick as we could be And ev - ery night drank

strong ba - shee, Says he you shall be my son - in - law And

mar - ry the Prin - cess Was - key Taw; Says I, your Ma - jes - ty,

hold your jaw, I will ac - cept the Prin - cess's paw.

Chorus:

With her Swan- go tan - go, ho - ki po - ki, hun - ky, dun - ky,

Ho - kee, po - kee, Pul - ka wul - ka, so - ki lo - ki,

All in the Ton - go Is - land,

All in the Ton - go Is - land.

2

My bride was fair as you'll suppose,
She had a feather through her nose
And had some rings upon her toes,
The pride of the Tongo Island.
A mat she had for a petticoat
And a string of scalps around her throat,
For she kill'd fifty chiefs of note
And did upon a battle dote.
Our wedding feast description flogs,
T'was in a palace built of logs.
We'd yam and blubber and twelve baked hogs
And by way of a dainty, some roasted dogs.
And our Swango tango, hoki poki, hunky, dunky,
Hokee, pokee, Pulka wulka, soki loki,
All in the Tongo Island,
All in the Tongo Island.

3

My wife a charming fair was she,
And we lived in great harmony
Till the chiefs they jealous grew of me,
All in the Tongo Island.
They swore they'd cut me up like pork,
And eat me without knife or fork,
Thinks I, why this is precious work,
And off my body I'd better walk.
So one fine morn to show my wit
Not being ready for the spit
To cut and run I did think fit.
Thus 'stead of biting they were bit,
And then Swango tango, hoki poki, hunky,
Hokee, pokee, Pulka wulka, soki loki,
All in the Tongo Island,
All in the Tongo Island.

The Tea Tax

By A Gentleman of Boston

2

And t'other day we Yankee folks were mad about the taxes
And so we went, like Indians dressed, to split tea chests with axes
I mean, t'was done in seventy-five, and we were real gritty
The mayor he would have led the gang, but Boston warn't a city.

3

Ye see we Yankees didn't care a pin for wealth or booty
And so in State Street we agreed we'd never pay the duty,
That is, in State Street 'twould have been, but 'twas King
        Street they called it then,
And tax on tea, it was so bad, the women wouldn't scald it
        then.

4

To Charleston Bridge we all went down to see the thing
        corrected,
That is, we would have gone there, but the bridge it warn't
        erected.
The tea perhaps was very good, Bohea, Souchong or Hyson
But drinking tea it warn't the rage, the duty made it poison.

5

And then we went aboard the ships our vengeance to administer,
And didn't care a tarnal curse for any king or minister;
We made a plaguy mess o' tea in one of the biggest dishes,
I mean, we steeped it in the sea and treated all the fishes.

And then you see we were all found out, a thing we hadn't
    dreaded,
The leaders were to London sent and instantly beheaded,
That is, I mean they would have been if ever they'd been taken,
But the leaders they were never cotch'd and so they saved their
    bacon.

Now Heaven bless the President and all this goodly nation
And doubly bless our Boston Mayor and all the corporation;
And may all those who are our foes, or at our praise have
    falter'd.
Soon have a change, that is I mean may all of them get haltered.

Analization

Sung by G. Andrews

What are mor – tals made of? By
an – al – iz – a – tion I've tried all the na – tion, De-
fined each gra-da – tion, in eve – ry sta – tion, With Sir
Hum – phry's best new che-mi – cal test, And
found what mor – tals are made of.

vivace

What are law - y - ers made of?

What are law - y - ers made of? Of

caus - es and fees, de - mur - rers and pleas,

Learn - ed broth-er and lots of pother,

Counsel and jur - y with very wise looks, Flaw in the in - dict-ment and

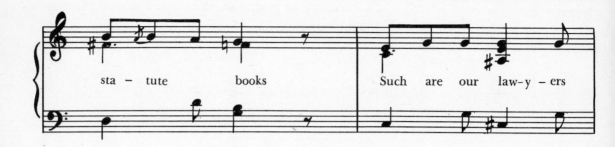

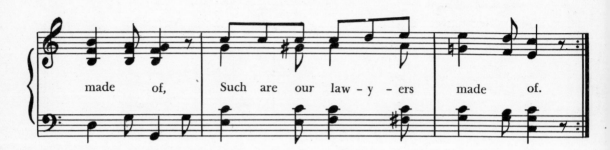

sta - tute   books   Such   are   our   law-y - ers

made   of,   Such   are   our   law - y - ers   made   of.

2

What are our old maids made of?
What are our old maids made of?
Of thrown away sighs, and crows' feet eyes,
Of sprigs of rue and vinegar too;
Parchment skin and faltering walk,
Chit chat and slander to talk;
And such are our old maids made of,
And such are our old maids made of.

3

What are old bacheldores made of?
What are old bacheldores made of?
Of bread and cheese and very weak knees,
Of snivelling nose and rheumatic toes.
Domestic comfort they say is all strife,
But yet in their hearts they all long for a wife;
And such are old bacheldores made of,
And such are old bacheldores made of.

4

What are New Yorkers made of?
What are New Yorkers made of?
Of State House in Park, Broadway in the dark,
Of ladies who flash and cut such a dash,
The home of the stranger, delight of the brave,
Lots of frolic and fashion and brokers that shav
And such are New Yorkers made of,
And such are New Yorkers made of.

5

What are Philadelphians made of?
What are Philadelphians made of?
Of dandies and Quakers and Germans and Shak
Of fine Schuylkill coal and shad by the shoal;
At the mint they make money, Oh lawks, what a
And the market it reaches for nearly a mile;
And such are Philadelphians made of,
And such are Philadelphians made of.

Bones and Tambo

AMERICAN BLACK-FACE COMEDY PERFORMANCES
are generally said to have begun with the famous performance of
Thomas D. Rice, often known as "Daddy," in 1832. This is probably
inaccurate, since there is definite evidence of negro-flavored comedy

101

songs before that date. Still Rice's performance was a landmark of a kind, and became proverbial.

Rice was fascinated by the manners of a shuffling old Nego whom he had observed, one who was called Jim Crow. He worked out a tune and verse, and made up a little act in which he imitated the black man's gestures. "Jump, Jim Crow" was a huge success. The words were on everybody's tongue, "Jim Crow" became synonymous with the entire Negro race, and to this day is used to designate the space allotted to Negroes in public places in those states where they are segregated.

They say that when Rice first did this act in Pittsburgh, he borrowed the ragged outfit of a Negro who was loitering in the theater at the time. The clothes were the only ones the man had, and he had to wait out in the cold while the performance was going on. The number was a "wow," as we now say, and there were any number of encores. Suddenly, the voice of the neglected Negro was heard from the wings: "Ah wants mah clothes!" The act thus ended with a little dividend of unintentional humor.

But Rice was really a soloist. We do not get a full-fledged minstrel show, so-called, until the formation of the "Big Four" early in the 1840's. Daniel D. Emmett, the immortal composer of "Dixie," was one of the guiding spirits of that group. Later on in the 50's, E. P. Christy organized a very successful troupe, which had the good fortune to present many of Stephen Foster's songs to the public for the first time. The idea spread and grew, and for the rest of the century the minstrel show was probably America's favorite type of popular stage entertainment.

A certain essential routine was developed in the minstrel shows. The troupe as a whole was a band of musicians seated in a semi-circle; its keystone was a central personage known grandly as the "interlocutor." Its lateral supports were the two "end men," the one at the right being known as "Bones," the one at the left as" Tambo." The word "Bones" was used because of an actual set of animal bones which the man rattled rhythmically, in the manner of castanets, and which he was also often skillful in juggling. "Tambo" is an abbreviation for "tambourine," famous hand and rattle-drum, also "playable" in several senses.

The jokes were usually steered by the interlocutor, who set up a manner of seriousness and dignity, which was regularly knocked down by the ribald cracks of one or the other of the "end men." Songs and dances, of course, were interspersed throughout the dialogue. The songs were largely humorous, though by no means always so.

Many of America's most esteemed actors served some time on the minstrel circuit, among them Joseph Jefferson, Edwin Forrest, Chauncey Olcott, Nat Goodwin and Otis Skinner.

In addition to the bones and the tambourine, the minstrels played various kinds of fiddles and horns; but the most celebrated instrument of all was the banjo. For quite a while it probably became America's most popular non-vocal source of music. Its origin is not certain. It has long been associated with Negroes, and may possibly have been brought over by them in some form from Africa. There is an African word "banjar" meaning a kind of gourd, over which strings may have been stretched and plucked. An early American song, published about 1820, calls the instrument a "bonja."

The minstrel shows were fundamentally the expression of states of mind of white people. It is true, the minstrels blacked their faces,

103

imitated and exaggerated Negro speech and posturing, but this was largely a mask for the utterance of white sentiments. After the 1870's, attracted by the profits of the business, groups of real Negroes entered the field with some success. But there was an essential lack of authenticity in these performances. Negroes giving a Negro minstrel show are, perversely enough, actually imitating white men.

Millions of people, however, enjoyed them just the same. Witness the popularity of Williams and Walker, or Cole and Johnson.

Jim Crow

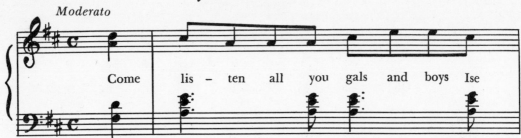

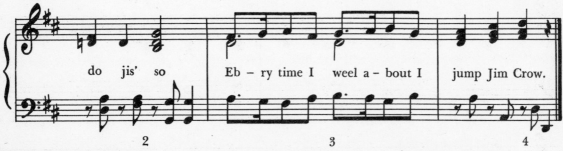

2	3	4
I went down to de river,	And arter I been dere awhile	I git upon a flat boat
I didn't mean to stay,	I t'ought I push my boat;	I cotch de Uncle Sam;
But dere I saw so many gals,	But I tumbled in de river	Den I went to see de place where
I couldn't get away.	An' I find myself afloat.	Dey killed de Packenham.

5	6
An' den I go to Orleans	When I got out I hit a man,
An' feel so full of fight;	His name I now forgot;
Dey put me in de calaboose	But dere was noting left of him
An' keep me dere all night.	'Cept a little grease spot.

Zip Coon

Pos – sum up a gum tree, coon– ey on a stump

Pos – sum up a gum tree, coon – ey on a stump

Pos – sum up a gum tree, coon – ey on a stump Den

ov – er dub – ble trub – ble Zip Coon will jump.

107

2

Oh, ole Sukey blueskin, she fell in lub with me,
Oh, ole Sukey blueskin, she fell in lub with me,
Oh, ole Sukey blueskin, she fell in lub with me,
She 'vite me to her house to take a cup o' tea.
What do you tink ole Sukey had for de supper
What do you tink ole Sukey had for de supper
What do you tink ole Sukey had for de supper
Chicken foot, sparrowgrass, applesauce butter.

3

I went down to Sandy Holler todder afternoon
I went down to Sandy Holler todder afternoon
I went down to Sandy Holler todder afternoon
And de fust man I met dare was ole Zip Coon.
Ole Zip Coon he is a natty scholar
Ole Zip Coon he is a natty scholar
Ole Zip Coon he is a natty scholar
Plays upon be banjo, "Cooney in de holler."

4

Did you ever see de wild goose sail upon de ocean?
Did you ever see de wild goose sail upon de ocean?
Did you ever see de wild goose sail upon de ocean?
O de wild goose motion is a very pretty notion;
Ebry time de wild goose beckons to de swaller
Ebry time de wild goose beckons to de swaller
Ebry time de wild goose beckons to de swaller
You can hear him google google, google google goller.

Turkey In The Straw   *To the tune of "Zip Coon"*

1

As I was a gwine on down de road
Wid a tired team and a heavy load
I cracked my whip and the leader sprung,
Says I, good-bye to the wagon tongue.

Chorus:
Turkey in the straw, Turkey in the hay,
Turkey in the straw, Turkey in the hay,
Roll 'em twist 'em up a high tuck-a-haw,
And hit up a tune called "Turkey in the Straw."

2

Went out to milk an' I didn't know how,
Milked the goat instead of the cow,
A monkey sittin' on a pile of straw,
Winkin' at his mother-in-law.

3

Met a big cat-fish comin' down de stream,
Says the big cat-fish "What does you mean
Caught the big cat-fish right on the snou
Turned Mister Cat-fish inside out.

The Camptown Races

By Stephen C. Foster

De Camp-town la – dies sing dis song Doo – dah!

doo-dah! De Camp-town race track five miles long Oh! doo-dah-

day! I come down dah wid my hat caved in

Doo-dah! doo – dah! I go back home wid a

pock- et full o' tin Oh! Doo- dah - day!

Chorus:

Gwine to run all night! Gwine to run all

day! I'll bet my mon-ey on de bob - tail nag

Some - bo - dy bet on de bay.

2

De long tail filly and de big black hoss—Doodah! doodah!
Dey fly de track and dey both cut across—Oh! Doodah-day!
De blind hoss sticken in a big mud hole—Doodah! doodah!
Can't touch bottom wid a ten foot pole—Oh! Doodah-day!

3

Old muley cow come on to de track—Doodah! doodah!
De bobtail fling her ober his back—Oh! doodah-day!
Den fly along like a railroad car—Doodah! doodah!
Runnin' a race wid a shootin' star—Oh! Doodah-day!

4

See dem flyin' on a ten mile heat—Doodah! doodah!
Round de race track, den repeat—Oh! Doodah-day!
I win my money on de bobtail nag—Doodah! doodah!
I keep my money in an ol' tow bag—Oh! Doodah-day!

Oh! Susanna

By Stephen C. Foster

Fast and spirited

I came from Al - a - bam - a wid my ban-jo on my knee, I'm g'wan to Lou - i - sian - a my true love for to see. It rained all night de day I left, the weath- er it was dry; The sun so hot I froze to death, Su - san - na don't you cry.

Chorus:

f Oh! Su - san - na, oh don't you cry for me, I've come from A - la - bam - a Wid my ban - jo on my knee.

2

I jumped aboard de telegraph and traveled down de river,
De 'lectric fluid magnified and killed five hundred nigger.
De bullgine bust, de hoss runs off, I really thought I'd die;
I shut my eyes to hold my breath, Susanna don't you cry.

3

I had a dream de odder night when ev'ry ting was still:
I thought I saw Susanna a-comin' down de hill.
De buckwheat cake war in her mouth, de tear was in her eye;
Says I, I'm comin' from de South, Susanna don't you cry.

4

I soon will be in New Orleans and den I'll look all round,
And when I find Susanna I'll fall upon de ground.
But if I do not find her, dis darkie'll surely die;
And when I'm dead and buried, Susanna don't you cry.

Polly-Wolly-Doodle

Oh, I went down South for to see my Sal, Sing Pol - ly — wol - ly - dood - le all day; My Sal - ly am a spun — ky gal, Sing Pol - ly - wol - ly - dood - le all day Fare thee well, fare thee

2

Oh, my Sal she am a maiden fair,
Sing Polly-wolly-doodle all day,
With curly eyes and laughing hair,
Sing Polly wolly-doodle all day,

3

Oh, I came to a river and I couldn't get across,
So I jumped on a nigga an' I thought he was a hoss,

4

Oh, a grasshopper sittin' on a railroad track,
A-pickin' his teeth wid a carpet tack,

5

Oh, I went to bed but it warn't no use,
My feet stuck out for a chicken roost,

6

Behind de barn down on my knees,
I thought I heard dat chicken sneeze,

7

He sneezed so hard wid de whoopin' cough,
He sneezed his head and tail right off,

Shoo Fly, Don't Bother Me

Chorus:

118

feel, I feel, I feel, I feel like a mor - ning star. I feel, I feel, I feel, I feel like a mor - ning star.

2

If I sleep in the sun, this nigger knows,
If I sleep in the sun, this nigger knows,
If I sleep in the sun, this nigger knows,
A fly come sting him on the nose.
I feel, I feel, I feel; that's what my mother said,
Whenever this nigger goes to sleep, he must cover up his head.

Noah's Ark

2

The animals went in one by one,
There's one wide river to cross!
And Japhet with a big bass drum,
There's one wide river to cross!

3

The animals went in two by two,
There's one wide river to cross!
The elephant and the kangaroo,
There's one wide river to cross!

4

The animals went in three by three,
There's one wide river to cross!
The hippopotamus and the bumble bee,
There's one wide river to cross!

5

When Noah found he had no sail,
There's one wide river to cross!
He just ran up his old coat tail,
There's one wide river to cross!

6

And as they talked on this and that,
There's one wide river to cross!
The ark it bunked on Ararat,
There's one wide river to cross!

7

Oh, Noah he went on a spree,
There's one wide river to cross!
And banished Ham to Afrikee,
There's one wide river to cross!

8

Perhaps you think there's another verse,
There's one wide river to cross!
But you'll soon find out that there ain't.
There's one wide river to cross!

Oh! Dem Golden Slippers

With spirit

Words and music by James A. Bland

Oh, my gold-en slip-pers am laid a-way, Kase I don't' spect to wear 'em till my wed-din'-day And my long-tailed coat dat I loved so well I will wear up in de cha-riot in de morn. And my

long white robe dat I bought last June I'm

gwine to get changed kase it fits too soon, And de

ole gray hoss dat I used to drive I will

hitch him to de char – iot in de morn.

Refrain:

Oh, dem gold-en slip-pers! Oh, dem gold-en slip-pers!

Gold-en slip-pers I'se gwine to wear be- kase they look so neat.

Oh, dem gold-en slip-pers! Oh, dem gold-en slip-pers!

Gold-en slip-pers I'se gwine to wear to walk de gold-en street.

2

Oh my ole banjo hangs on the wall
Kase it ain't been tuned since way last fall,
But de darks all say we will hab a good time
When we ride up in de chariot in de morn.
Dere's ole Brudder Ben and Sister Luce
Dey will telegraph de news to Uncle Bacco Juice;
What a great camp-meetin' dere will be dat day
When we ride up in de chariot in de morn.

3

So it's good-bye children I will have to go
Whar de rain don't fall and de wind don't blow,
And yer ulster coats, why yer will not need
When yer ride up in de chariot in de morn.
But yer golden slippers must be nice and clean
And yer age must be just sweet sixteen,
And yer white kid gloves yer will have to wear
When yer ride up in de chariot in de morn.

Antimacassar

MACASSAR IS A CITY IN CELEBES, IN THE DUTCH
East Indies. It used to export an oil to Europe, probably made of
cocoanut, which formed an important constituent of hair pomades
used by polite people of the nineteenth century. Housewives of the

126

more genteel sort used to pin little doilies called antimacassars, on the backs of their plush parlor chairs and settees, to protect them from the greasy caresses of the slickened coiffures.

Plush-protection, physical and spiritual, was much on the minds of the well-to-do among the Victorians. Rarely used living-rooms were stuffed full of elaborate hangings, and then kept in utter darkness during the day, lest the sunlight fade some of the colors. Expensively made upholstery surfaces were completely hidden from view, swathed in slip covers all summer long. All sorts of objects were manufactured; bowls, tables, fire-irons, that were meant to be looked at but not used. The ostentatious attitudes of our great-grandparents have often been written about, usually with too much animosity.

The outstanding product of Victorian culture was the young lady, herself. If the young children, the parents and the male members of the family were its leaves, roots and stems, the young adult unmarried daughter was its blossom. Rigorously sheltered from the necessity of making a living, all excess personal ambition discouraged, she could devote her entire time and thought to the cultivation of the niceties of petty demeanor and appearance, to being an exemplification of chaste and elegant daintiness; a living advertisement of the refinement, the prestige and the financial solidity of her parents.

The pruderies of the age are all too well known: how proper young ladies were expected to seem ethereally unconscious of bodily realities, not admitting the existence, in words, of belly, blood or sweat, and accepting legs only obliquely when they were masked as "limbs."

Sports for women, under these circumstances, were pretty much out of the question. Yet after the middle of the century the movement

127

for healthful exercise was growing. A compromise was found for the girls in the shape of a recreation known as croquet. It was a tame and friendly pastime, a sort of outdoor parlor game; it was eminently suitable to the cooperation of both men and women—pardon me—ladies and gentlemen—as well as children, and could well be played, though hardly played well, in a hoopskirt.

The song, "Croquet," given in this volume, dates from the earlier days of the game's vogue, and may have been thought of as slightly risqué in its day.

Music, of a sort, was much engaged in in Victorian homes; it was regarded, within certain restrictions, as a particularly becoming activity for young ladies. Musical life centered around the drawing-room piano, usually a square model, with heavy carved or turned legs, and the keyboard set in unequally between the two sides. A vast toast literature of young-lady music was manufactured and paid for by young ladies' fathers. Seventy-seven thousand "Maiden's Prayers" and "Last Hopes" fluttered from seven hundred and seventy thousand agony-boxes.

The songs were mostly on the viscously sentimental side. All the better if they could "move" the audience, that is: arouse suggestions of tears. Dead babies, blind boys, dear old decrepit grandparents, fallen soldiers, tombstones and goings to heaven were frequent objects of lyrical expression, and of course, "love" of a strictly decorous kind.

But being "moved" apparently did not include being moved to laughter. There was mistrust, at first, of permitting very many humorous songs within the hallowed family circle. One editor of an old songster completely and expressly omits them, alleging that comic songs were unsuited to the sensibilities of delicately brought up young females. The comic tended to be associated with the vulgar, perhaps not altogether incorrectly. Once you encourage the slightest vulgarity, it may soon degenerate into lubricity, and, horrors, into obscenity! A pure young girl could never even seem to admit knowledge of the existence of an unchaste thought.

Still, numbers of prettily humorous songs did find their way on to the domestic interiors of the genteel. We offer a few samples; they are strongly feminine in viewpoint, and quite lady-like. That is, all except the one called "The Gal with the Balmoral." That seems a bit too rude for here. It was the "balmoral" that prompted its inclusion. That appears to have been a woolen striped garment fashionable in the third quarter of the century.

I Can't Make Up My Mind

Allegretto—Polka rhythm

I can't make up my mind, Ma - ma, In
such un - seem-ly haste, Nor pick from all my
dy - ing swains A hus - band to my taste. There's
gay Charles Dash, a charm-ing man, Most af - fa - ble and kind, Who
loves me so de - vot - ed - ly, But I can't make up my mind.

2

And, next, there's frank young Harry West,
So fond, so true, so clever,
Who, though I scold him all the day,
Adores me more than ever.
There's Roger Snipe, the pink of beaux,
Or else your daughter's blind,
And yet when Snipe grows serious,
I can't make up my mind.

3

There's lawyer Keen, and poet Good,
Exemplars of their sort;
Still, still I can't make up my mind
There's no accounting for't!
"Yes, yes, there is," stern truth replied;
"Your vanity imparts
That false delight in flatt'ring tongues,
Which forfeits loving hearts."

4

On purpose, to make up her mind,
So long this fair one tarried,
Her lovers, loathe to hang themselves,
Sought other maids and married!
And, though Mama is growing old,
Her daughter looks much older,
E'er since her coquetry and pride
In the Old Maids' Corps enroll'd her.

Pray Papa

By P. K. Moran

"Pray Pa-pa, pray Pa-pa, stay a lit-tle long — er.

Pray Pa-pa, pray Pa-pa, do not go so soon."

2

"Your partner must excuse you
'Twon't break his heart to lose you,
And if you look so cross at him,
I'm sure you'll be no loss to him,
So pray bid him good-night,
You must be home by daylight."
"Pray Papa, pray Papa, stay a little longer.
Pray Papa, pray Papa, do not go so soon."

3

"This comes of dissipation,
Do have some moderation;
If you are so importunate,
You'll never make your fortune at
These balls and jigs and races
No matter what your face is."
"Pray Papa, pray Papa, stay a little longer.
Pray Papa, pray Papa, do not go so soon."

4

"The horses are but old ones,
The nights are very cold ones,
The coachman he is drunken,
You know the road is sunk in,
I'm sure the coach is calling,
And here they've brought your shawl in!"
"Pray Papa, pray Papa, stay a little longer.
Pray Papa, pray Papa, do not go so soon."

5

"Your Grandpapa is gouty,
He cannot do without you,
He takes the *eau medicinale*,
Not fit we should be missing all,
Your family is regular,
Indeed, child, I must beg you'll hear."
"Pray Papa, pray Papa, stay a little longer.
Pray Papa, pray Papa, do not go so soon."

6

"Indeed, Papa, so kind you've been,
To keep you longer were a sin,
The fiddlers they are half asleep,
And now the day begins to peep
And after dancing all the night
By daylight I shall look a fright.
"Pray Papa, pray Papa, don't stay a moment longer.
Pray Papa, pray Papa, let us haste away."

The Lords of Creation Men We Call

Allegretto

The Lords of cre - a - tion men we call, And they

think they rule the whole; But they're much mis - tak - en

af - ter all, For they're un - der Wo - man's con - trol.

f As ev - er since the world be - gan It has

al - ways been the way, For did not Ad - am, the

2

Ye Lords, who at present hear my song,
I know you will quickly say:
"Our size's more large, our nerves more strong;
Shall the stronger the weaker obey?"
But think not tho' these words we hear
We shall e'er mind the thing you say;
For as long as a woman's possessed of a tear
Your power will vanish away.

3

Now, Ladies, since I've made it plain
That the thing is really so,
We'll even let them hold the rein,
But we'll show them the way to go;
As ever since the world began
It has always been the way,
And we'll manage it so that the very last man
Shall the very last woman obey.

Croquet

Words by C. H. Webb
Music by J. R. Thomas

said   to   my - self, "Soon we'll   see   Cro – quet,   we'll

see   Cro –   quet."

2

But the Mallet and Balls unheeded lay,
And the maid and the youth side by side sat they,
And I thought to myself—
Is that Croquet?
I saw the scamp, it was bright as day,
Put his arm around her waist in a loving way,
And he squeezed her hand—
Was that Croquet, Was that Croquet?

3

While the red rover roll'd all forgotten away,
He whisper'd all that a lover should say,
And kiss'd her lips—
What a queer Croquet!
Silent they sat 'neath the moon of May,
But I knew by her blushes she said not nay,
And I thought in my heart,
Now that's Croquet! Now that's Croquet.

The Gal with the Balmoral

Words by Fred Wilson
Music by R. J. Herrero

wore a Bal - mo - ral.

Chorus:

O, there's fun up - on the ice, And

2nd time *pp*

lots of nice young gals, My good-ness how they

glide a - long, Dressed in their Bal - mo - rals.

2

We took a car and reach'd the park,
A man stood at the gate;
He charged us fifteen cents apiece,
To let us in to skate;
I paid the dimes and in we went,
With such a rush pell-mell
It beat my time to keep in track
Of that same Balmoral.

3

She started off and said she'd kiss,
The man that first would catch her;
Of all the folks upon the ice,
There's only one could match her.
I made a grab and down I went,
Upon my nose I fell;
Some other fellow caught and kiss'd
Her in the Balmoral.

4

My face was cut, my nose did bleed,
I was in such a plight;
I turned around to look for her,
But she was out of sight;
The young folks laugh'd and told me how,
She took that other swell
And ever since I faint away
To see a Balmoral.

140

Heinie and Mick

WHAT IS FUNNY ABOUT A FOREIGN ACCENT?
Probably about the same thing that is funny about a hare lip—to
some people. A man trying for something he cannot quite get is likely
to arouse laughter; or tears, if the matter is made to seem important

enough. Until recently, accents have not been regarded seriously enough to make us refrain from taking them humorously.

It stands to reason that a nation which used to welcome the humblest of strangers to its shores and conferred the benefit of its citizenship upon them after a mere five years' residence would be strongly infiltrated by people whose relationship to the American language was, to say the least, familiar without being authentic. Furthermore, the foreigners gave themselves away immediately upon opening their mouths, and that tended to make them readily classifiable, as types. There have been many kinds of these foreign accents, or "dialects" as they are miscalled, in the United States. But the best known and the longest prevalent have been the German and the Irish.

The Irish came in large numbers during the middle of the nineteenth century. Poor people from a poor country, they had little opportunity to develop skills. Heavy manual labor was what most of them had to put between themselves and hunger; some with native shrewdness found it useful in city politics. They enjoyed dangerous trades, such as railroading and pugilism.

The "respectable" Anglo-Saxon Americans did not treat them with unmixed kindness. "Hit him again, he's Irish," was a phrase that used to float around. Apparently, certain employers used to discriminate against them. A song appeared during the 50's called "No Irish Need Apply." In it a girl protests against the title-slogan, and says that those are shabby words to use to the compatriots of Robert Emmett and Wolf Tone. "I used to think when I was a boy," said a typical Connecticut gentleman, "that Catholicism was a superstitious kind of caricature of Christianity chiefly indulged in by ignorant Irish servant girls." This is a rather vivid expression of what many people felt about the Hibernian immigration. On the whole genteel Yankees then considered the Irish newcomers to their cities much as they now consider their present-day Latin and Slavonic equivalents.

But the Irishmen made a familiar place for themselves in American life. Everybody got to know Irish hod-carriers, Irish washerwomen and Irish policemen. The song "Drill, Ye Tarriers, Drill!" deals with the Irish as construction workers. The word tarrier apparently means a laborer.

Inevitably the Irish came to be shown and caricatured on the stage, and to have songs written about them. Half of all the funny yarns passed around used to be about Pat and Mike. Lots of third rate humor could get by if it were needled with a little "dialect." Irish music came to have a familiar ring. Songs like "St. Patrick's Day" and "Garyone" (miscalled "Garry Owen") became household tunes. They were both included by Vieuxtemps, the famous Belgian violin virtuoso, in his paraphrases of American melodies. "Garyone" became the favorite tune of General Custer's army when it fought the Indians in Wyoming.

The stage Irishman became a conventionalized type, though not entirely unrealistic. All the brogue artists were by no means genuine natives of Ireland. In the show business the words "Irish comedian" were the name of an effect, not necessarily of an essence. It was a trade name, something like "mahogany" or "seal." The Irishman was generally portrayed as a desperate romanticist, with an unlimited appetite for physical violence and for hard liquor.

The song "Down Went McGinty" presents an interesting study in emotional attitudes on the part of the public. It tells of a man whose impulsiveness leads him into a series of dreadful misfortunes, ultimately resulting in his suicide. Truly a tragic story. The more adult-minded public of today would probably see it as such; and the fact that McGinty always wore his best suit of clothes, when he broke his bones, fell down a coal-hole, went to jail and jumped in the sea, would add to the poignancy of the tale. But fifty years ago the song was thought of as comic. It is unlikely that it would have been had the hero not been Irish.

The most popular Irish comedians of their time were the team of Harrigan and Hart. Their vogue flourished for a couple of decades beginning shortly after the Civil War. It was they who first introduced the song "The Mulligan Guards." After the War the martial spirit remained active for a number of years. Amateur rifle clubs were organized in many cities. However, many of their meetings and picnics apparently degenerated into drinking parties. "The Mulligan Guards" was a show satirizing this state of affairs, and the song was its hit number. The chorus is a delightful tune, but not very Irish. In fact it sounds suspiciously Viennese. The Avenue A of the song is a proletarian street in Manhattan's extreme East Side.

The specifically Irish strain has all but faded out of American life. The descendants of the wearers of the green now speak straight American, and have intermarried with other stocks; few of them carry hods or pickaxes. The famous brogue has all but disappeared from the stage, in fact it might now be difficult to find an actor who could imitate it properly. Pat and Mike stories have a quaintly old-fashioned corny flavor, even among traveling salesmen.

It may sound strange to one whose memory does not go back

beyond World War I, but it is none the less true that, historically, the German, on the whole, was looked upon by the Yankee with a kindlier eye than was the Irishman. He was obstinately and mistakenly called a Dutchman, but that was not so represensible an error, seeing that that was almost what he called himself. Anyway, the German was never really confused with the Netherlander, who was often referred to as "Holland Dutch."

A certain orderly industriousness, a disinclination for drunken brawls, a general similarity of his family customs to those of the Anglo-Saxons made him an acceptable-seeming immigrant. But the "Dutch" and the Irish rarely get on well together.

Much German lore was readily and generally adopted in the United States. Several German songs were naturalized at an early date, for instance: "Silent Night" and "O Tannenbaum," which most Americans know as "Maryland, My Maryland." The little German band enlivened many a holiday street.

The German's food was the object of some good-humored ridicule at first. Sauerkraut and sausage were long-standing subjects of pleasantries; so were pretzels. There was an erroneous idea that Limburger cheese was a German product, probably caused by the confusing use of the word "Dutch." Anyway, Limburger is still a laughing matter. The deepest impression of all, however, made by anything German, was that produced by his beer. For a nation which teetered morbidly between a lurid craving for fiery liquor and an equally neurotic abhorrence of all alcoholic beverages, the German's mild tipple must indeed have seemed interesting and peculiar. The Yankees laughed for a while, but they accepted all these things. Weiners, sauerkraut, pretzels and lager beer are now 100 percent American products.

145

As a stage type, the German fared less well, on the whole, than the Irishman. He was not so picturesque, to begin with. Usually he was represented as a phlegmatic simpleton, often the victim of some absurd discomfiture.

Of the songs given here, the tune of "The Dutch Warbler" is taken from a well-known German ditty called "In Lauterbach hab' ich mein' Strumpf verloren." There is a suggestion of a yodel in the chorus.

"Johnny Schmoker," with naive recapitulations of past verses, has its effect much enhanced if it is performed with illustrative gestures and noises.

Dutch Warbler (or Der Deitcher's Dog)

Easy going waltz

Words by Sep Winner

Oh where, oh where ish mine lit - tle dog gone, Oh

where, oh where can he be? His

ears cut short and his tail cut long. Oh

where, oh where ish he?

REFRAIN:

tra, la la la, la la la, la la la

la, la la la la la la, la la la

la, tra, la la la, la la la, la la la

la, la la la, la la la la!

148

2

I loves mine lager, tish very goot beer,
Oh where, oh where can he be?
But mit no money I cannot drink here,
Oh where, oh where ish he?

3

Across the ocean in Germanie,
Oh where, oh where can he be?
Der Deitcher's dog is der best companie,
Oh where, oh where ish he?

4

Un sausage is goot, bolonie of course,
Oh where, oh where can he be?
Dey makes um mit dog and dey makes um mit horse,
I guess dey makes um mit he.

Johnny Schmoker

by George F. Root

2

Johnny Schmoker, Johnny Schmoker, ich kan spielen, ich kan spielen,
Ich kan spiel' mein kleine Fifie.
Pilly-willy-wink mein kleine Fifie,
Rub-a-dub-a-dub mein kleine Drummel.
Mein rub-a-dub-a-dub, mein pilly-willy-wink mein kleine Fifie.

3

Johnny Schmoker, Johnny Schmoker, ich kan spielen, ich kan spielen,
Ich kan spielen mein Triangel.
Tic toc knock das ist mein Triangel,
Pilly-willy-wink mein kleine Fifie,
Rub-a-dub-a-dub mein kleine Drummel.
Mein rub-a-dub-a-dub, mein pilly-willy-wink, mein tic toc knock mein klein Triangel.

4

Johnny Schmoker, Johnny Schmoker, ich kan spielen, ich kan spielen,
Ich kan spiel' mein kleine Trombone.
Boom boom boom mein kleine Trombone,
Tic toc knock mein klein Triangel,
Pilly-willy-wink mein kleine Fifie,
Rub-a-dub-a-dub mein kleine Drummel.
Mein rub-a-dub-a-dub, mein pilly-willy-wink, mein tic toc knock, mein boom boom boom das ist mein Trombone.

5

Johnny Schmoker, Johnny Schmoker, ich kan spielen, ich kan spielen,
Ich kan spiel' mein kleine Cymbal.
Zoom zoom zoom mein kleine Cymbal,
Boom boom boom mein kleine Trombone,
Tic toc knock mein klein Triangel,
Pilly-willy-wink mein kleine Fifie,
Rub-a-dub-a-dub mein kleine Drummel.
Mein rub-a-dub-a-dub, mein pilly-willy-wink, mein tic toc knock, mein boom boom boom, mein zoom zoom zoom das ist mein Cymbal.

6

Johnny Schmoker, Johnny Schmoker, ich kan spielen, ich kan
　　spielen,
Ich kan spiel' mein kleine Viol.
Fa la la mein kleine Viol,
Zoom zoom zoom mein kleine Cymbal,
Boom boom boom mein kleine Trombone,
Tic toc knock mein klein Triangel,
Pilly-willy-wink mein kleine Fifie,
Rub-a-dub-a-dub mein kleine Drummel.
Mein rub-a-dub-a-dub, mein pilly-willy-wink, mein tic toc knock,
　　mein boom boom boom, mein zoom zoom zoom, mein fa la
　　la mein kleine Viol.

7

Johnny Schmoker, Johnny Schmoker, ich kan spielen, ich kan
　　spielen,
Ich kan spiel' mein kleine Toodle-Sach,
Whack whack whack mein kleine Toodle-Sach.
Fa la la mein kleine Viol,
Zoom zoom zoom mein kleine Cymbal,
Boom boom boom mein kleine Trombone,
Tic toc knock mein klein Triangel,
Pilly-willy-wink mein kleine Fifie,
Rub-a-dub-a-dub mein kleine Drummel.
Mein rub-a-dub-a-dub, mein pilly-willy-wink, mein tic toc knock,
　　mein boom boom boom, mein zoom zoom zoom, mein fa la
　　la la, main whack whack whack mein kleine Toodle-Sach.

The above is the complete exact sequence of the words of this
song. If it is sung from the condensed form given with the
notes, it may be done as follows:
　　1. All verses begin with section A.
　　2. First verse ends with end of section B.
　　3. In section B all verses after verse 1 are recapitulated in
reverse order, for example: 4, 3, 2, 1.
　　4. All verses after verse 1 conclude with section D.

The Teuton's Tribulation

Quite a moderate pace

By A. Dodge

Mine Cot! Mine Cot! Vot lan-guage dot I can—not Eng-lish sprak-en; For shust so sure I speak him right So sure I bees mis-tak-en. For

ven I say I want my *beer* I mean dot lag – er
fix – en, *Bier* means dem tings folks
ride up – on Ven dey go dead as blix – en.

2

Meat means dem tings dat coot to eat,
Meet also means tings proper;
It's only *mete* to measure tings,
Ven steamboats *meet* dey stopper.
Shust de same vord means everytings,
It makes no business vether
You spell him did or todder vay,
Von sound shust like de todder.

The Mulligan Guards

Vigorous march time, especially the chorus

Words by Edward Harrigan
Music by David Braham

155

Guards.   We   Guards.

2

When the band played Garry Owen or the Connemara Pet,
We'd march in the mud with a rub-a-dub-dub in the military
  step.
With Green above the Red, boys, to show where we'd came from,
Our guns we'd lift with a right shoulder shift as we marched
  to the beat of the drum.

3

When we got home at night, boys, the divil a bite we'd ate,
We'd all sit up and drink a sup of whisky strong and nate;
Then we'd all march home together as slippery as lard,
The solid men would all fall in and march with the Mulligan
  Guard.

Down Went McGinty

By Joseph Flynn

Sunday morning just at nine, Dan Mc-Ginty dressed so fine, Stood looking up at a ver-y high stone - wall; When his friend young Pat Mc-Cann, says, "I'll bet five dol-lars, Dan, I could car - ry you to the top without a fall." So on his shoulders he took Dan, to climb the lad - der he be-gan, And

soon commenced to reach up near the top; When Mc-

Gin- ty, cute old rogue, to win the five he did let go, Nev-er

think- ing just how far he'd have to drop.

Chorus:

Down went Mc-Gin-ty to the bot-tom of the wall, And

tho' he won the five, he was more dead than a-live, Sure his

159

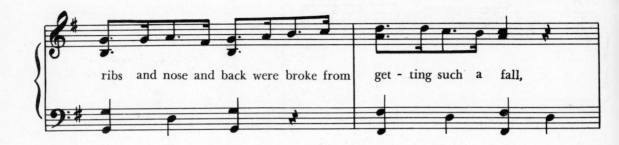

ribs and nose and back were broke from get-ting such a fall,

Dress'd in his best suit of clothes.

2

From the hospital Mac went home, when they fixed his broken
    bones,
To find he was the father of a child;
So to celebrate it right, his friends he went to invite,
And soon he was drinking whisky fast and wild;
Then he waddled down the street in his Sunday suit so neat,
Holding up his head as proud as John the Great;
But in the sidewalk was a hole, to receive a ton of coal,
That McGinty never saw till just too late.

Chorus:

Down went McGinty to the bottom of the hole,
Then the driver of the cart gave the load of coal a start
And it took us half an hour to dig McGinty from the coal,
Dress'd in his best suit of clothes.

3

Now McGinty raved and swore, about his clothes he felt so sore,
And an oath he took he'd kill the man or die;
So he tightly grabbed his stick and hit the driver a lick,
Then he raised a little shanty on his eye.
But two policemen saw the muss and they soon joined in the fuss,
Then they ran McGinty in for being drunk;
And the Judge says with a smile, we will keep you for a while
In a cell to sleep upon a prison bunk.

Chorus:

Down went McGinty to the bottom of the jail,
Where his board would cost him nix, and he stay'd exactly six;
They were big long months he stopp'd for no one went his bail,
Dress'd in his best suit of clothes.

4

Now McGinty thin and pale, one fine day got out of jail,
And with joy to see his boy was nearly wild;
To his house he quickly ran to see his wife Bedaley Ann,
But she skipp'd away and took along the child.
Then he gave up in despair and he madly pulled his hair
As he stood one day upon the river shore;
Knowing well he couldn't swim, he did foolishly jump in,
Although water he had never took before.

Chorus:

Down went McGinty to the bottom of the say (sea)
And he must be very wet for they haven't found him yet,
But they say his ghost comes round the docks before the **break**
    of day,
Dress'd in his best suit of clothes.

You're in the Army Now

S.M.Adler

THE QUESTION IS, WHAT CONSTITUTES AN ARMY
song? During our national crises our army consists of a huge number
of transmogrified civilians. They like to sing the same songs they sang
before they put on their uniforms. Many of these have nothing to do

with war or fighting or soldiering. During the days of the American Expeditionary Force in 1917 to 1919, songs like "There's A Long, Long, Trail," "Smiles" and "K-K-K-Katy" were enthusiastically taken up by the armed forces and became associated with it, but they are nostalgic, sentimental or humorous songs that the army happened to like, not really army songs. No future historian could ever find anything military about them merely from their content.

The same holds true for "There'll be a Hot Time in the Old Town Tonight," the great hit of the Spanish-American War of 1898, even though the bands played it so much that many of the Cubans and Spaniards, they say, thought it was our national anthem!

Then there are patriotic songs, composed by civilians, that are sung in the camps; for instance "Over There," or "Marching Through Georgia." Strictly speaking they are not army songs either, even though they deal with the purpose for which the army is raised.

The real army and navy songs are those that originate in the services themselves. They are rarely sentimental or patriotic. They treat of the every day details of the soldier's work and play. "Caissons" is a true army song; it has acquired a patriotic flavor by association, but it really only speaks of the movement of vehicles, a technical matter. Actually army and navy songs are more like work songs; they talk about the hard labor, the difficult climate, the pay, the food, the supposed easy life of the bosses, the awkwardness of the recruits and the girls with whom they might become temporarily acquainted when on leave.

Most of them have a salty, even sardonic humor. Occasionally the life seems to be more than the singer can bear, and he wails: "I Don't Want No More Army." But real deserters would hardly sing about it in advance. The Navy has an equivalent "No Navy for Me" not given here.

The songs we have assembled here are mostly of the genuine type we have described. However, we have included a few that fall outside our criterion of classification, such as "Captain Jinks of the Horse Marines" and "A Capital Ship." They have nothing to do with the Army or Navy, or with fighting either, for that matter, but they have been sung in the services, they contain military and naval references and they are very amusing. Both of them, incidentally, originated in England. The English have been great virtuosos in the art of concocting nonsense, and the tale of the walloping widow blind is a masterpiece in their best tradition.

"The Regular Army, Oh!" did not originate in the army either, but its spirit is much akin to that of the authentic service songs. It began as a Harrigan and Hart number shortly after the Civil War. The regular, that is, professional army as distinguished from the citizens' Grand Army of the Republic which was disbanded after the War, offered the kind of life that appealed to many Irishmen, and many of its ranks were filled with them. Thus it made a good subject for the famous comedians' specialty. The Army took up the song, and it is said to have been sung by the men who were in the Indian fights in the west during the 70's. Note the reference to Arizona in one of the later verses. The tune is superb and has a strong Irish favor. It would be worth reviving as a march today.

"Mister, Here's Your Mule" is from the Confederate Army, few of whose songs are heard much today. The song recounts what is alleged to have been an actual occurrence in one of the camps.

Few people will miss the point of having "The Rookie" set

164

to the tune of "Reuben and Rachel." The latter are supposed, judging from their names, to be a truly rural couple; and this conforms to the notion that the raw recruit's simplicity of mind is supposed to be that of a hayseed.

"You're in the Army Now" has the distinction of being a bugle call, a song, and a proverb all at the same time. It began as a bugle corps march: the words given are supposed to be the traditionally correct ones. But the song is a great favorite, and new racy verses are continually being added to it.

"If You Want to Know Where the Privates Are," "Hinky Dinky Parley Voo" and the "Hearse Song" were all much sung by the A.E.F. during the first World War.

The first is a military version of proletarian envy; the second is the most famous and exhibits a great relish for certain soldierly adventures not in the line of duty. Hundreds of roving verses of the ditty exist, endless naughtiness has been strung out with it. It is hard to say why anything so gruesome as the "Hearse Song" should seem humorous; yet most people will probably feel that it is. The song is said to have been a special favorite with the airmen. Perhaps they saw the silly face of death more distinctly than the others.

"Farewell to Grog," is a memento of September 1, 1862, on which date the regular liquor ration to men of the U.S. Navy was abolished. The song is said to have been composed and sung with much hilarity the night of August 31. Its composer was Caspar Schenk, U.S.N.

"The Monkeys Have No Tails in Zamboanga" was sung by the sailors, marines and soldiers who helped to pacify the Philippines early in the 1900's. Zamboanga, Mindanas, Mariveles and other such names are localities in the Islands in which the comforts of home were apparently conspicuously absent. Some of the men were fortunate enough to be able to go north, that is to China, in the spring.

The Regular Army, Oh!

March time

Three years a-go. this ver-y day I
went to Gov-nor's Isle To stand fern-inst the
can-non in true mil-it-ar-y style; Thir-
teen Am-er-i-can dol — lars each month we sure-ly
get To car-ry a gun and bay-on-et with a

168

2

We had our choice of going to the army or to jail,
Or it's up the Hudson River with a cop to take a sail;
So we puckered up our courage and with bravery we did go,
And we cursed the day we marched away with the Regular
    Army, oh!

3

The captain's name was Murphy, of "dacint French descint,"
Sure he knew all the holy words in the Hebrew testament:
And when he said to Hogan: "Just move your feet a foot,"
Sure, Hogan jumped a half a mile on Sergeant Riley's boot.

4

The best of all the officers is Second Lieutenant McDuff;
Of smoking cigarettes and sleep he never got enough.
Says the captain, "All we want of you is to go to Reveille,
And we'll let the first sergeant run the company."

5

There's corns upon me feet, me boy, and bunions on me toes,
And lugging a gun in the red hot sun puts freckles on me nose,
And if you want a furlough to the captain you do go,
And he says, "Go to bed and wait till you're dead in the Regular
    Army, oh!"

6

We went to Arizona for to fight the Indians there;
We were nearly caught bald-headed but they didn't get our hair;
We lay among the ditches in the dirty yellow mud,
And we never saw an onion, a turnip or a spud.

7

We were captured by the Indians and brought ferninst the chafe;
Says he, "We'll have an Irish stew," the dirty Indian thafe.
On the telegraphic wire we skipped to Mexico,
And we blessed the day we marched away from the Regular
    Army, oh!

Mister, Here's Your Mule

Swinging rhythm

A farm-er came to camp one day, With

milk and eggs to sell, Up-on a mule that

oft would stray To where no one could

tell. The farm-er tir-ed of his tramp, For

hours was made a fool By ev-'ry one he

met in camp With, "Mis - ter, here's your mule."

Chorus:

Come on, come on, come on, old man, And

don't be made a fool By ev - 'ry one you

meet in camp With, "Mis - ter, here's your mule."

2

His eggs and chickens all were gone,
Before the break of day;
The mule was heard of all along,
That's what the soldiers say,
And still he hunted all day long,
Alas! a witless tool,
Whilst ev'ry man would sing the song,
Of, "Mister, here's your mule."

3

Alas, one day the mule was miss'd!
Ah; who could tell his fate?
The farmer like a man bereft,
Search'd early and search'd late,
And as he passed from camp to camp,
With stricken face—the fool,
Cried out to ev'ry one he met,
"Oh, Mister, where's my mule?"

Captain Jinks of the Horse Marines

With an easy swing

I'm Cap - tain Jinks of the Horse Ma - rines, I feed my horse on corn and beans, And sport young la - dies in their teens Tho' a Cap - tain in the Arm- y. I teach the la - dies how to dance, How to dance, how to dance; I

teach the la - dies how to dance For I'm the pet of the Arm - y.

Refrain:

I'm Cap - tain Jinks of the Horse Ma - rines, I feed my horse on corn and beans, And of - ten live be - yond my means Tho' a Cap - tain in the Arm - y.

2

I joined my corps when twenty-one,
Of course I thought it capital fun;
When the enemy comes of course I run,
For I'm not cut out for the Army.
When I left home, mamma she cried,
Mamma she cried, mamma she cried,
When I left home, mamma she cried,
"He's not cut out for the Army."

3

The first time I went out for drill
The bugler sounding made me ill,
Of the battlefield I'd had my fill
For I'm not cut out for the Army.
The officers they all did shout,
They all did shout, they all did shout,
The officers they all did shout,
"Why, kick him out of the Army!"

I Don't Want No More Army

Slowly

The of-fic-ers live on top of the hill; We live down in the

slop and swill I don't want no more arm - y.

Lord - y, how I want to go home!

2
They showed me the mule that I could ride;
They didn't show the shovel on the other side—
I don't want, etc.

3
We've got a kitchen on four wheels,
Just a-warming beans for our meals—

4
I've learned a little, more or less;
Now I know why they call it mess—

5
The meat was rotten, and the spuds were bum;
They mixed it all together and they called it slum—

6
We had a major and his name was Tack;
He rode a horse and we carried a pack—

7
The lieutenants they all work and sweat;
The captain sits around like a violet—

8
We loaded up the wagon and then
We had to take it all off again—

9
The officers they don't work a bit;
I don't see how they get away with it—

10
We do work for the lieutenant, and then
The captain makes us do it all over again—

You're in the Army Now

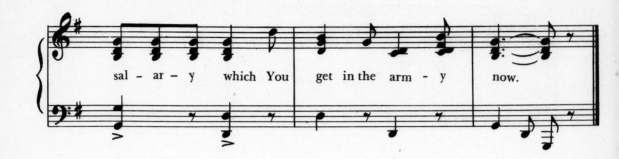

sal - ar - y   which You   get in the arm - y   now.

If You Want to Know Where the Privates Are

March time

If you want to know where the priv – ates are, I'll tell you where they are, I'll tell you where they are, yes! I'll tell you where they are. If you want to know where the priv – ates are, I'll tell you where they are: Up to their necks in

mud!   I   saw

them,   I   saw   them,

Up   to their   necks   in   mud,   I   saw   them,

Up   to their   necks   in   mud!

2

If you want to know where the sergeants are,
I'll tell you where they are,
I'll tell you where they are, yes!
I'll tell you where they are.
If you want to know where the sergeants are,
I'll tell you where they are:
Drinking up the privates' rum!
I saw them, I saw them,
Drinking up the privates' rum, I saw them,
Drinking up the privates' rum!

3

If you want to know where the captains are,
I'll tell you where they are,
I'll tell you where they are, yes!
I'll tell you where they are.
If you want to know where the captains are,
I'll tell you where they are:
Down in the deep dugout!
I saw them, I saw them,
Down in the deep dugout, I saw them,
Down in the deep dugout!

4

If you want to know where the colonels are,
I'll tell you where they are,
I'll tell you where they are, yes!
I'll tell you where they are.
If you want to know where the colonels are,
I'll tell you where they are:
Playing with mademoiselles!
I saw them, I saw them,
Playing with mademoiselles, I saw them,
Playing with mademoiselles!

5

If you want to know where the majors are,
I'll tell you where they are,
I'll tell you where they are, yes!
I'll tell you where they are.
If you want to know where the majors are,
I'll tell you where they are:
Way behind the lines!
I saw them, I saw them,
Way behind the lines, I saw them,
Way behind the lines!

6

If you want to know where the generals are,
I'll tell you where they are,
I'll tell you where they are, yes!
I'll tell you where they are.
If you want to know where the generals are,
I'll tell you where they are:
Back in gay Paree!
I saw them, I saw them,
Back in gay Paree, I saw them,
Back in gay Paree!

The Rookie

Tune: *Reuben and Rachel*

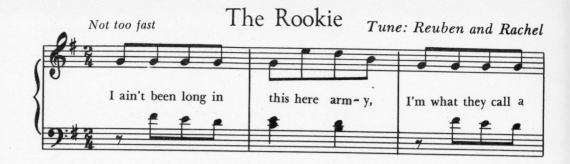

I ain't been long in this here arm-y, I'm what they call a

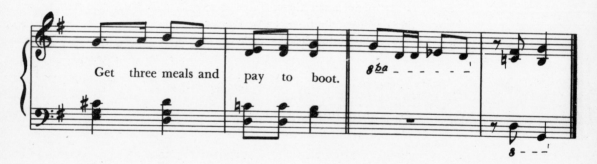

raw re-cruit. Guess I'll stay, it's bet-ter than farm-in'

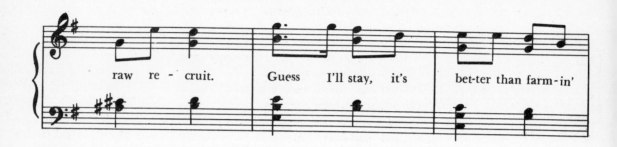

Get three meals and pay to boot.

2
The very first thing in the morning
Fellow with a horn makes an awful noise.
Then the guy they call first sergeant
Says, "Get up and turn out, boys."

3
Then you go down to the bath house,
Place like that I never saw before.
Water runs in through a hole in the ceiling,
Runs right out through a hole in the floor.

4
They tried to learn me a soldier lesson,
Marched me up and turned me round.
Give me a gun and put it on me shoulder,
One two three an' I put it on the ground.

5
They put your name on a piece of paper,
Fellow over there gives you your pay.
Take it to the squad room, put it on a blanket,
Fellow yells "CRAPS" an' takes it all away.

6
Then they try to talk by signals,
Fellow waves a flag to one far away.
Just one thing I'm trying to get over—
How he knows what he's tryin' to say.

7
Then if you should get your leg broke
Doctor won't charge you one red cent.
"C.C." pills is all you need;
Your leg ain't broke, just badly bent.

Hinky Dinky, Parley-Voo?

March time

Mad - e - moi - selle from Ar - men - tieres, par - ley - voo? Mad - e - moi - selle from Ar - men - tieres, par - ley - voo? Mad - e - moi - selle from Ar - men - tieres, She had-n't been kissed in man - y years, Hin - ky din - ky,

par - ley - voo?

2

Mademoiselle from gay Paree, parley-voo?
Mademoiselle from gay Paree, parley-voo?
Mademoiselle from gay Paree,
You certainly did play hell with me.
Hinky dinky, parley-voo?

3

Landlord, have you a daughter fair
To wash a soldier's underwear?

4

Mademoiselle from St. Nazaire,
She never heard of underwear.

5

The French they have some customs rare,
They sit and drink in the public square.

6

The French they are a funny race,
They fight with their feet and save their face.

7

The American soldier on the Rhine
Kissed the women and drank the wine.

8

The general got the Croix-de-guerre,
The son of a gun was never there.

9

The M.P.s say they won the war
Standing on guard at a cafe door.

10

You might forget the gas and shell,
You'll never forget the mademoiselle.

11

Many and many a married man
Wants to go back to France again.

Hearse Song

Like a funeral march

Have you ev – er thought as the hearse goes by That

one of these days you will sur – e – ly die? They'll

take you a – way in that big black hack, They'll

bur – y you deep and you won't come back.

Epilogue ad lib

2

The old gray hearse goes rolling by,
You don't know whether to laugh or cry,
For you know some day it'll get you too
And the very next load may consist of you.

3

They'll take you out, they'll lower you down,
The men with shovels will stand around;
They'll shovel in dirt and they'll shovel in rocks
And they won't give a damn if they break the box.

4

The worms'll crawl in and the worms'll crawl out,
They'll crawl all over your chin and mouth,
They'll invite their friends and relatives too,
And you'll look like hell when they're through with you.

5

Your eyes'll drop out and your teeth'll fall in,
The worms'll crawl on your mouth and chin,
Then each one takes a bite or two
Out of what the war office used to call you.

A Capital Ship

Fast with spirit

A cap-it-al ship for an oc - ean trip, Was the *Wal-lo-ping Win-dow Blind!* No wind that blew dis-mayed the crew, Or troubled the cap - tain's mind; The man at the wheel was made to feel Con - tempt for the wil-dest

blow,   Tho' it   of - ten ap-peared, when the

gale had cleared, That he'd been   in his bunk be - low.

Chorus:

Then   blow, ye winds, heigh - ho!   A   rov - ing I will

go!   I'll   stay   no   more on   Eng-land's shore, So

let the mus – ic play! I'm off for the mor – ning train! I'll cross the rag – ing main! I'm off to my love with a box-ing glove, Ten – thousand miles a – way!

2

The bos'n mate was very sedate,
Yet fond of amusement too;
He played hopscotch with the starboard watch,
While the captain, he tickled the crew!
And the gunner we had was apparently mad,
For he sat on the after rail,
And fired salutes with the captain's boots,
In the teeth of the booming gale!

3

The captain sat on the commodore's hat,
And dined in a royal way,
Off toasted pigs and pickles and figs
And gunnery bread each day;
And the cook was Dutch and behaved as such,
For the diet he gave the crew,
Was a number of tons of hot cross buns
Served up with sugar and glue.

4

We all felt ill as mariners will,
On a diet that's cheap and rude,
And we shivered and shook as we dipped the cook,
In a tub of his gruesome food;
Then nautical pride we laid aside,
And we ran the vessel ashore,
On the Gulliby Isles where the Poopoo smiles,
And the rubbly Ubdugs roar.

5

Composed of sand was that favored land,
And trimmed with cinnamon straws,
And pink and blue was the pleasing hue
Of the tickle-tie-toaster's claws;
And we sat on the edge of a sandy ledge
And shot at the whistling bee,
And the cinnamon bats wore waterproof hats,
As they dipped in the bounding sea.

6

On the Rugby bark from morn till dark,
We dined till we all had grown
Uncommonly shrunk, when a Chinese junk
Came up from the Torribly zone;
She was chubby and square, but we didn't much care,
So we cheerily put out to sea,
And we left all the crew of the junk to chew
On the bark of the Rugby tree.

What Are You Going To Do
With A Drunken Sailor?

What are you going to do with a drunk-en sail-or?

What are you go-ing to do with a drunk-en sail-or?

What are you go-ing to do with a drunk-en sail-or?

Ear - ly in the mor - ning!

Chorus: Fast

High, high, *Slow* up she ris - es!

(Last chorus followed by a slow "Amen.")

2

Put him in a boat and row him over,
Put him in a boat and row him over,
Put him in a boat and row him over,
Early in the morning!

3

Put him in the brig until he's sober,
Put him in the brig until he's sober,
Put him in the brig until he's sober,
Early in the morning!

4

Hoist him up to the topsail yardarm,
Hoist him up to the topsail yardarm,
Hoist him up to the topsail yardarm,
Early in the morning!

5

Make him turn to at shining bright work,
Make him turn to at shining bright work,
Make him turn to at shining bright work,
Early in the morning!

6

Make him clean out all the spit-kits,
Make him clean out all the spit-kits,
Make him clean out all the spit-kits,
Early in the morning!

7

That's what you do with a drunken sailor,
That's what you do with a drunken sailor,
That's what you do with a drunken sailor,
Early in the morning!

Farewell to Grog

Chorus after each verse.

By Caspar Schenk, U.S.N.

Not too fast, but briskly

Come, mess – mates, pass the bot – tle 'round, Our time is short, re – mem – ber, For our grog must stop, and our spir – its drop, On the first day of Sep – tem – ber.

Chorus:

For to – night we'll mer – ry, mer – ry be, For to – night we'll mer – ry, mer – ry be, For to – night we'll

mer - ry, mer - ry be, To - mor - row we'll be sob - er.

2

Farewell old rye, 'tis a sad, sad word,
But alas! It must be spoken,
The ruby cup must be given up,
And the demijohn be broken.

3

Jack's happy days will soon be gone,
To return again, oh never!
For they've raised his pay five cents a day
But stopped his grog forever.

4

Yet memory oft' will backward turn,
And dwell with fondness partial,
On the days when gin was not a sin,
Nor cocktails brought court-martial.

(Bo's'n-mates pipe "All Hands Splice the Main Brace.")

5

All hands to split the main brace, call,
But split it now in sorrow,
For the spirit-room key will be laid away
Forever, on to-morrow.

Zamboanga

Allegretto

Oh, the mon-keys have no tails in Zam-bo-an - ga.
Oh, the mon-keys have no tails in Zam-bo-
an - ga, Oh, the mon-keys have no
tails, They were bit-ten off by whales, Oh, the
mon-keys have no tails in Zam-bo - an - ga.

2

Oh, the carabao have no hair in Mindaneo,
Oh, the carabao have no hair in Mindaneo,
Oh, the carabao have no hair,
Holy smoke! But they are bare,
Oh, the carabao have no hair in Mindaneo.

3

Oh, the birdies have no feet in Mariveles,
Oh, the birdies have no feet in Mariveles,
Oh, the birdies have no feet,
They were burned off by the heat,
Oh, the birdies have no feet in Mariveles.

4

Oh, we'll all go up to China in the spring time,
Oh, we'll all go up to China in the spring time,
Oh, we'll hop aboard a liner,
I can think of nothing finer,
Oh, we'll all go up to China in the spring time.

5

Oh, we'll all go down to Shanghai in the fall,
Oh, we'll all go down to Shanghai in the fall,
Oh, we'll all get down to Shanghai,
Those champagne corks will bang high,
Oh, we'll all go down to Shanghai in the fall.

6

Oh, we lived ten thousand years in old Chefoo,
Oh, we lived ten thousand years in old Chefoo,
And it didn't smell like roses,
So we had to hold our noses,
Oh, we lived ten thousand years in old Chefoo.

Brow's Sweat

S. M. Adler

SINGING AT WORK IS ONE OF THE OLDEST HABITS
of mankind. Music is a muscle stimulant, so what more natural than
for men to make up their own shots-in-the-arm while they needed
them? It is hard to see how the dreadful chore of building the Egyptian

pyramids could have ever been completed unless the workmen could have coordinated their movements by some kind of singing. But there are other kinds of work songs, songs about work, but not necessarily accompanying it. They may deal with the hardness of the toil, the injustice of the boss, the hazards of the job, and such perennial themes.

In the United States various groups of working men—railroad men cowboys, lumberjacks, miners and sailors—developed their own special songs. As long as they had the benefit of a certain amount of isolation, they could build them into a tradition. As long as the conditions of work remained the same, and opportunities for outside music scarce, they would continue to hand down the same song for a long time. But conditions changed quickly in this dynamic society. The old songs could not keep on living. They spoke of things that had ceased to exist; tools changed, jobs changed, whole types of industry became obsolete. Communications became fluid; why bother with some old and meaningless ditty when you can have a nice brand new one, expertly sung, at the touch of a button? And if any of the young miners, sailors or railroad workers seem to show any creative musical talent, let them try to chisel into Tin Pan Alley or Hollywood and cash in on it, rather than waste their talents on a limited or local audience. So many of the older work songs have gone out of use and are revived mostly by students.

The cowboy songs, however, have enjoyed a somewhat artifically prolonged twilight. They originated during the days of 1860 - 1890, when there were still large tracts of unfenced free grazing-land in the west. Smaller private owners of cattle drove their stock over great distances in search of grass, and the songs may well have helped break the monotony of these long journeys. The rise of large corporations, the spread of railroads and the fencing-in of the free range changed the nature of the cattle business and the songs lost much of their original reason for existence.

However, the romance of the west has established a tremendous hold on the American imagination. Endless fiction is still being commercially manufactured about a land that has long since passed into the fourth dimensions. But even if Americans know that the world of Indian fights, desperadoes, indiscriminate pistol practice, wild riding and secret gold mines is no more, they still like to dream about it. So the cowboy songs are carrying on a nostalgic after-life. Dude ranches help preserve it. There are now professional cowboy singers.

As for the content of these songs, their atmosphere has been well expressed by Sarah D. Lowrie in an often quoted statement: "There was one joke—a fall from a horse; one sorrow—a lonely grave; one temptation—cutting loose in a prairie town; one business—getting the little dogies back and forth to new lands."

The following explanations may prove useful:

The words: lasso, lariat, reata, maguey, twine, seago and gutline all mean the same thing. They are designations of the chief tool of the cowboy's trade, his rope. A "hole in the old seago" is a coil in his rope.

A "dogie" is a young calf, possibly a yearling who is not very strong or an orphan. The o is long as in "go," the g is hard as in "buggy."

A "slick ear" is a calf that has not yet been earmarked.

A "swallow fork" means clipping a piece out of a calf's ear in the shape of a swallow's tail.

The name of the bad horse of the song "Zebra Dun" probably

is a corruption of the name of the ranch to which the horse belonged: Z-Bar, "Dun" means dun-colored.

Believe it or not, the railroads, those staid work horses of today, once were things of glamor. A hundred, eighty, even sixty years ago they were thrilling fountains of speed and power; they stepped up the eight miles an hour of the horse-and-buggy to an almost unimaginable thirty or forty; they churned up an awesome violence as they flung their massive tonnage past the puny observer; their portentous choo-choo and the menacing crescendo of their approach evoked a fascinating terror. They were not safe; that was part of their lure; they sparkled with the danger that is in all true romance. Boys and men vibrated to them with ardor, as they now do to airplanes. There was adventure in railroads in those days, unlike today when they maintain schedules with monotonous regularity and do not even have to boast any longer of their safety, but prate instead of their soft matresses and their Spanish Omelets. No longer are they much fun to work on, to ride in, or even to speculate with.

There were many wrecks in those days; they had a kind of epic quality, to be cherished in song and story. For a long time the town of Ashtabula, Ohio, was chiefly known for the fact that a passenger train once keeled over an embankment near there.

Of course there were songs about railroads and the people who built and ran them, their hazards, excitements and tribulations. "Casey Jones" is the best remembered. There are the usual confusions about its origin. It was plausibly claimed that the song was rather recent, that Casey Jones was a real person, that the wreck described actually took place in southern Illinois about 1900. In fact a monument has been erected to commemorate it. On the other hand there is evidence to show that even if all this be so, the song is an adaptation of a ballad of earlier days. It is sung in many different versions. In some of them the hero is called K. C. Jones, perhaps for Kansas City, a large railroad center.

It may seem strange to include this vivid account of death and destruction in a collection of humorous songs; but there is that whimsical last line which tilts the whole thing on one ear. Mrs. Jone's nonchalant proclamation of the existence of an available man-power reserve recalls the once prevalent and no doubt scurrilous notion that a railroad wife's domestic life might be as irregular as her husband's absences from home. But probably that was all part of the romance of the rails!

"Paddy Works on the Railroad" reflects the fact that the Irish were well represented as laborers in the early days of railroad construction, as indeed they were in many other mascular occupations. The tune, too, has a fundamentally Celtic flavor.

The high point of railroad fever came during the building of the Union Pacific and its transcontinental connections. Built from both ends, Irish workmen from the eastern side vied for speed with Chinese from the west, until the golden spike was triumphantly hammered in at Ogden, and for the first time in history an entire continent was nailed down in steel. But who knows any of the Chinese songs?

Rusty Jiggs and Sandy Sam

Not too fast

A - way up high in the Sir - ey Peaks, Where moun - tain pines grow tall, San - dy Sam and Rus - ty Jiggs Had a round - up camp last fall.

2
They had their ponies and their running irons
And maybe a dog or two,
And they 'llowed they'd brand every slick-eared dogie
That came within their view.

3
Now every old dogie with long flop ears
That didn't hole up by day,
Got his long ears trimmed and his old hide scorched
In the most artistic way.

4
Says Sandy Sam to Rusty Jiggs
As he threw his seago down,
"I figures I'm tired of cowpography
And reckons I'll go to town."

5

So they saddled their ponies and struck a lope,
For it was quite a ride,
But them was the days when an old cowpunch
Could wet his dry inside.

6

Well, they started in at Kentucky Bar
Up at the head of the row,
And ended up at the Depot House
Just seventy drinks below.

7

As they was a-coming back to camp
A-carrying that awful load,
Who should they meet but the Devil himself,
A-walking down the road.

8

Says the Devil to them, "Now you cowpunching skunks,
You'd better hunt your holes,
For I've come up from the rim-rocks of Hell
To gather in your souls."

9

"The Devil be damned," says Sandy Sam,
"Though I know that we are tight,
No Devil ever killed an old cowpunch
Without one hell of a fight."

10

So he built him a hole in his old seago
And he threw it straight and true,
And he caught the Devil by both horns,
And he had it anchored too.

11

Now Rusty Jiggs was a reata man
With his gut-line coiled neat,
So he shook it out and he built him a hole,
And he snared that Devil's hind feet.

12

So they stretched him out and they tailed him down,
And they got their irons red hot,
And they put a swallow fork in each ear
And they scorched him up a lot.

13

Then they left him there in the Sirey Peaks,
Necked up to a big black oak,
Left him there in the Sirey Peaks,
Tied knots in his tail for a joke.

14

Now if you're ever up in the Sirey Peaks,
And you hear one helluva wail,
You'll know that it's the Devil himself
Cryin 'bout the knots in his tail.

Zebra Dun

March time

1

We was camped on the plains at the head of the Cimarron,
When along came a stranger and stopped to argue some.
He looked so very foolish, we began to look around,
We thought he was a greenhorn just escaped from town.

2

He said he'd lost his job upon the Santa Fe,
Was going 'cross the plains to strike the Seven D.
He didn't say how come it, some trouble with the boss,
But asked if he could borrow a fat saddle hoss.

3

This tickled all the boys to death, they laughed in their sleeves.
"We will lend you a fine hoss, fresh and fat as you please."
Shorty grabbed a lariat and roped the Zebra Dun
And give him to the stranger and waited for the fun.

4

Old Dunny was an outlaw, had grown so awful wild
He could paw the moon down, he could jump a mile,
Dunny stood right still as if he didn't know,
Until he was saddled and ready for to go.

5

When the stranger hit the saddle, Dunny quit the earth,
And traveled right straight up for all that he was worth,
A-pitching and a-squealing and a-having wall-eyed fits,
His hind feet perpendicular, his front feet in the bits.

6

We could see the tops of the mountains under Dunny's every
    jump,
But the stranger was growed there like the camel's hump.
The stranger sat upon him and curled his black moustache
Like a summer boarder waiting for the hash.

7

He thumped him in the shoulders and spurred him when he
    whirled,
And hollered to the punchers, "I'm the wolf of the world."
And when he had dismounted once more upon the ground
We knew he was a thoroughbred and not a gent from town.

8

The boss who was standing 'round watching at the show,
Walked up to the stranger and said he needn't go,
"If you can use the lasso like you rode old Zebra Dun,
You're the man I'm looking for since the year one."

9

There's one thing and a sure thing I've learned since I've been
    born,
Every educated feller ain't a plumb greenhorn.

Great Grandad

Great Gran - dad when the West was young

Barred his door with a wag - on tongue, For the

times were rough and the red - skins mocked, And he

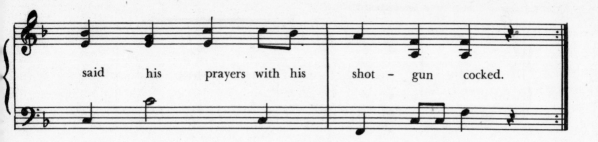

said   his   prayers with his   shot - gun   cocked.

Interlude

2
Great Grandad was a busy man,
He cooked his grub in a fryin' pan;
He picked his teeth with his huntin' knife,
And wore the same suit all his life.

3
He was a citizen tough and grim,
Danger was duck soup to him;
He eat corn pone and bacon fat,
But his great grandson would-a starved on that.

4
Twenty-one children came to bless
The old man's home in the wilderness;
But great Grandad he didn't lose heart,
For the dogs hunted rabbits and they
    ketched right smart.

5
Twenty-one boys and not one bad;
But they didn't get fresh with their old Grandad,
For if they had he'd-a been right glad
Just to tan their hides with a hickory gad.

6
Twenty-one boys and tall they grew,
Strong and fat on the bacon too;
They slept on the floor with the dogs and cats,
And they hunted in the woods
    fer their coonskin caps.

7
He raised 'em rough and he raised 'em well.
When their feet took hold of the road to hell
He filled 'em full of the fear of God,
And straightened 'em out with his old ramrod.

8
They grew strong of heart and hand,
The firm foundation of this land.
Twenty-one boys, but his great grandson
Is having a hell of a time with one.

Paddy Works on the Railroad

Briskly, one beat to a measure

In eigh - teen hun - dred and for - ty -
wan I put me cor - d'roy breech - es
on, I put me cor - d'roy breech - es
on, To work up - on the rail - way.

Chorus:

Fil - i - me - oo - re - i - re - ay,

Fil - i - me - oo - re - i - re - ay,

Fil - i - me - oo - re - i - re - ay, To

work up - on the rail - way.

2

In eighteen hundred and forty-two,
I left the ould world for the new,
Bad cess to the luck that brought me through,
To work upon the railway.

3

When we left Ireland to come here,
And spend our latter days in cheer,
Our bosses they did drink strong beer,
And Pat worked on the railway.

4

Our contractor's name it was Tom King,
He kept a store to rob the men,
A Yankee clerk with ink and pen,
To cheat Pat on the railway.

5

It's "Pat, do this" and "Pat, do that,"
Without a stocking or cravat,
And nothing but an old straw hat,
While Pat works on the railway.

6

In eighteen hundred and forty-three,
'Twas then I met sweet Biddy Magee,
And an illygant wife she's been to me,
While workin' on the railway.

7

In eighteen hundred and forty-six
I was in a hell of a fix,
I changed my trade to carrying bricks
From working on the railway.

Casey Jones

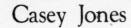

Seriously, but not too slowly

Come all you rounders if you want to hear A

stor - y 'bout a brave en - gin - eer,

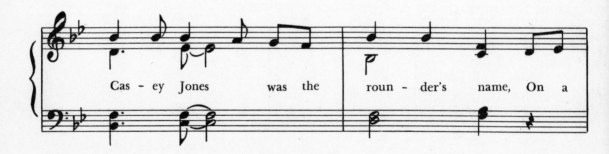

Cas - ey Jones was the roun - der's name, On a

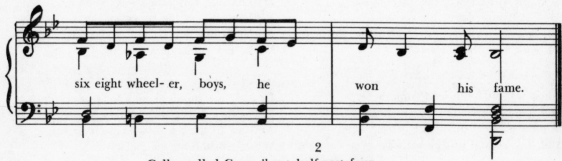

six eight wheel- er, boys, he won his fame.

2

Caller called Casey 'bout half-past four,
He kissed his wife at the station door;
Climbed to the cab with his orders in his hand,
He says: "This is my trip to the holy land."

3

The rain was comin' down five or six weeks,
The railroad track was like the bed of a creek;
They slowed her down to a thirty-mile gait
And the south-bound mail was eight hours late.

4

Fireman says, "Casey, you're runnin' too fast
You run that block board the last station you passed."
Casey says, "I believe we'll make it though,
For she steams a lot better than I ever knows."

5

Around the curve and down the dump,
Two locomotives were bound to bump,
Fireman hollered, "Casey, it's just ahead
We might jump and make it but we'll all be dead."

6

Around the curve comes a passenger train
Casey blows the whistle, tells the fireman "Ring the bell!"
Fireman jumps and says "Good-bye
Casey Jones, you're bound to die."

7

Mrs. Jones was a sittin' on the bed
Telegram comes that Casey is dead.
She says, "Children, go to bed, and hush your cryin'
'Cause you got another papa on the Frisco line."

Cape Cod Chanty

Lustily

Cape Cod girls they have no combs Heave a-way, heave a-way! They comb their hair with cod-fish bones; We are bound for Au-stra-lia!

Chorus:

Heave a-way my bul-ly bul-ly boys, Heave a-way, heave a-way; Heave a-way and don't you make a noise, We are bound for Au-stra-lia!

2

Cape Cod boys they have no sleds
    Heave away, heave away!
They slide down hill on codfish heads,
We are bound for Australia!

3

Cape Cod cats they have no tails,
    Heave away, heave away!
They blew away in heavy gales,
We are bound for Australia!

4

Cape Cod roosters never crow,
    Heave away, heave away!
And crowing hens are all the go.
We are bound for Australia!

Whiskey, Johnny

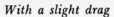

With a slight drag

Whiskey is the life of man,

Whis-key, John-ny! I'll drink whis-key

while I can, Whis-key for my John-ny!

2

Whiskey from an old tin can,
Whiskey, Johnny!
I'll drink whiskey when I can,
Whiskey for my Johnny!

3

I drink it hot, I drink it cold,
Whiskey, Johnny!
I drink it new, I drink it old,
Whiskey for my Johnny!

4

O whiskey straight and whiskey strong,
Whiskey, Johnny!
Give me whiskey and I'll sing you a song,
Whiskey for my Johnny!

5

Whiskey makes me feel so sad,
Whiskey, Johnny!
Whiskey killed my poor old dad,
Whiskey for my Johnny!

6

Whiskey makes me wear old clothes,
Whiskey, Johnny!
Whiskey gave me a broken nose,
Whiskey for my Johnny!

7

If whiskey comes too near my nose,
Whiskey, Johnny!
I tip it up and down she goes,
Whiskey for my Johnny!

8

I had a girl, her name was Lize,
Whiskey, Johnny!
She puts whiskey in her pies,
Whiskey for my Johnny!

9

My wife and I cannot agree,
Whiskey, Johnny!
She puts whiskey in her tea,
Whiskey for my Johnny!

10

Here comes the cook with the whiskey can,
Whiskey, Johnny!
A glass of grog for every man,
Whiskey for my Johnny!

11

A glass of grog for every man,
Whiskey, Johnny!
And a bottle full for the shantyman,
Whiskey for my Johnny!

Love, Food and Stuff

S. M. Adler

MOST OF THE SONGS ARE ABOUT LOVE; LOVE
hoped for, love gained, love lost. Even love unsighted, as in "Gee, I
wish that I had a girl, like the other fellows have." Fair enough. But
after love, what? First, there are the old reliable objects of lyrical

feeling; homesickness, God, and country. After that, most anything. Americans, in particular, have never found anything they hesitated to sing about. Food and drink, work and entertainment, clothing fashions, fads and crazes, new inventions, political situations, economic conditions, spectacular accidents, domestic relations—anything.

Almost anything that happened could inspire a song, and as the music business became more systematically commercialized, topical songs were expressly written and timed for the market. Back in 1850, we find a song about the "Jenny Lind Mania," lampooning the flurry that celebrated song-bird created on her American tour. Soon we find songs about greenbacks, about hard times; long ago there was one called "Calomel," poking fun at the doctor's rock of ages. We have them about amateur rifle clubs, about the transatlantic cable, the telephone, about bicycles built for two, and precarious automobiles from which one had to get out and get under. There was one about a cat who always came back, about the man who broke the bank at Monte Carlo. There was one which said that everybody worked but father, and another about a man who could dance with anybody but his wife. As prohibition spilled its fog over us, we were made to sing hopefully: "I'll See You in C-U-B-A." Still later we had a quintuplets' lullaby.

It would be an exaggeration to claim that one could reconstruct the factual history of the United States from a study of its songs alone. Yet they often throw significant sidelights on the people's states of mind and their emotional attitudes. They will be an invaluable source material for the archeologists of the future, should enough copies be spared by the ravages of accident, war and neglect.

We are giving a rather random aggregation of miscellaneous

216

songs in these pages, which makes no pretension of being anything more than a sampling.

So far as food is concerned: the Negro is usually supposed to be notable for his whole-hearted enjoyment of simple physical pleasures. So we find that the favorite Negro bill-of-fare is quite well represented in song: there is possum and taters, watermelon, chicken, ham, and short'nin' bread. Most of the songs given here are probably minstrel rather than really Negro. But "Short'nin' Bread" seems to have the authentic touch. It concerns a bread in which pork fat has been baked right into the dough.

The white man also likes to eat well enough to sing about it. "Goober peas" is a southern word for peanuts, and the cheerful little Confederate army ditty that goes by that name reflects the universal pleasure given by that most American of comestibles. Then too, Cousin Jedediah's relatives, all christened piously at random from the Old Testament, all eager to impress him, among other things, with a turkey accompanied by "pan dowdy." Apparently this is a kind of pastry that New Englanders liked to eat with roasts; perhaps it is something like Yorkshire pudding.

The American people were much devoted to the circus during the latter half of the nineteenth century. Suitable as it was to the tastes of men, women and children of all classes and races, it probably was America's most widely enjoyed form of entertainment. What is more natural than that people should sing about the institution that made P. T. Barnum famous? And that added the concepts of "Siamese Twins" and "Wild Man of Borneo" to the language.

Concerning liquor: vocally speaking, during the nineteenth century, liquor's enemies were much more active than its friends.

217

Most of the liquor songs are of the temperance variety. One stands aghast at their number. Lists of twenty or thirty appear in the music store catalogues of the 1860's. They became a regular commercial line. The temperance societies, Sunday schools, and revival meetings apparently had an insatiable demand for new versions of the old propaganda. They never seemed to find one good enough to stick to for long, except perhaps H. C. Work's "Come Home, Father." There even exists a temperance parody on the "Star Spangled Banner."

By contrast, liquor's friends are, it stands to reason, better tempered and more humorous than its enemies. Furthermore, they have no illusions about the way their fetish requites their devotion:

> *It's you who makes my friends my foes,*
> *It's you who makes me wear old clothes!*

says the bard of the "Little Brown Jug."

During the early years of the present century the boll weevil, an insect from Mexico, crept across the border, and despite heroic efforts to combat it, within a number of years destroyed a large part of many cotton crops. The "Ballard of the Boll Weevil," is a gallows-humorous Negro version of this calamity. Some people profited, if only in experience, from the depredations of the bug; it gave a terrible object lesson on the danger of too great a reliance on a single crop. At any rate so thought one small Southern town, which erected a monument to the boll weevil.

The "Darky Sunday School" Bible-jazzing was, of course, never thought up by a Negro. But it may have been inspired by the vivid realism with which many Negroes envision the events of the sacred Scriptures. The reference to John L. Sullivan may help roughly to date the song. That famous boxer and slugger was word's heavyweight

218

champion during the 1880's, holding his title until 1893. The glamor of his name lasted more than two decades longer.

"Musieu Bainjo" originated with the French-speaking Negroes of the Gulf Coast.

Petroleum was described by Marco Polo as far back as 1290, but it took nearly six hundred years before anybody ever did anything about it. It was right after the Civil War that the Pennsylvania and Ohio wells were beginning to be exploited, and that the foundations for some of the country's most famous fortunes, including that of the Rockefellers, were being laid. New holes were drilled, new companies formed, new hopeful money allured. The country was off on one of those get-rich-quick orgies it has loved so well. There were several songs about the speculation fever of those days, one "Have Ye Struck Ile?" being contemporaneous with "Oil on the Brain" given here. Wonder what ever became of all those companies mentioned in the last verse?

"Jeff in Petticoats" takes advantage of one of those unkind rumors that are so easy to spread during war times. In 1865 thousands of Northerners believed, and their newspapers encouraged them, that Jefferson Davis, President of the defeated Confederate States of America, upon being pursued by the victorious Union Army, attempted to escape capture by disguising himself in his wife's clothing. It pleased many people to be able to think of their enemy in a ridiculous and disgraceful situation. The story was a malicious invention based on the shred of fact that when Mr. Davis came out of his tent to meet his captors, his wife had placed a shawl over his shoulders to protect him from the evening chill, thus giving him a vaguely feminine silhouette.

"Kingdom Comin' " was written by Henry C. Work, gifted song writer, ardent abolitionist and Union sympathizer, and member of the music-publishing firm of Root and Cady of Chicago. "Marching Through Georgia" was another outstanding product of his talents. Next to his more famous colleague, Stephen Foster, he was probably the ablest of our mid-century popular composers. Unlike Foster, Work was a well-adjusted personality, had a happy family life, did not die too young, and made himself a comfortable income from his abilities, thus making less claim on the belated sympathy of posterity.

"Kingdom Comin'" is supposed to depict the joy of Negro slaves when their masters left them to go to war. It was a minstrel song and was, of course, first sung by blacked-up white men. There may have been Negroes who echoed the song's sentiments. It is a mighty good tune in any case.

Good Sweet Ham

Moderately

Words and Melody by Henry Hart

You may talk a – bout good eat – ing, Of your oys – ters and your chow-dered clam, But it's when I'm aw – ful hung-ry, Then just give me good old sweet ham. Now some folks may dif – fer with me, But their talk is noth-ing but a sham, For to touch this dar – kie's pa – late, Oh just

If you want to see good living,
Just go down to the cabins mongst the palm,
And it's there you'll see the children
Greas'd all over with old sweet ham;
Now the possum is good eating,
When it's cooked with taters call'd the yam;
But there's nothing yet that suits me
Just as well as good old sweet ham.

3

Now my song is almost ended
And you all know who this darkey am,
For the boys have all nicknamed me
By them calling me old sweet ham.
I am going back to the old home,
There to pass my life away in calm,
And if you should hear I'm dead . . .
Then just lay it to old sweet ham.

Short'nin' Bread

2

Went to de kitchen, kicked off de led,
Fill up my pocket full o' short'nin' bread.
Put on de skillet and put on de led,
My lil' baby wants short'nin' bread.

3

One little darkie lyin' in bed,
When he hear tell of de short'nin' bread,
Pop up so lively and he dance an' sing,
Almos' cut 'em de pigeon wing.

Hie Away Home

Not fast

Anonymous "Plantation" Song

226

Chorus:

Hie a-way home, hie a-way home, There's trou-ble all a-bout so you'd bet-ter watch out: Hie a-way home, hie a-way home, Hie a-way, hie a-way home.

2

Sometime chicken gets de whoopin' cough
Hie away, hie away home.
The doctor has to take him off,
Hie away, hie away home.
Put him on a spit and roast him sweet,
It's hard to beat dat chicken meat;
Eat him all except de feet,
Hie away, hie away home.

Eating Goober Peas

Walking time

Sit - ting by the road - side on a sum - mer day, Chat - ting with my mess-mates, pass- ing time a - way, Ly - ing in the shad-ow un - der - neath the trees, Good-ness, how del - ic - ious, eat-ing goob-er peas!

Chorus:

Peas! Peas! Peas! Peas! eat - ing goob - er peas!

228

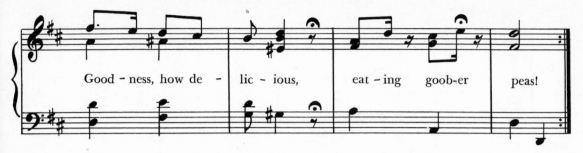

Good - ness, how de - lic - ious, eat - ing goob-er peas!

2

When a horseman passes the soldiers have a rule,
To cry out at their loudest, "Mister, here's your mule";
But another pleasure enchantinger than these,
Is wearing out your grinders, eating goober peas!

3

Just before the battle the Gen'ral hears a row,
He says, "The Yanks are coming, I hear their rifles now."
He turns around in wonder, and what do you think he sees?
The Georgia Militia, eating goober peas!

4

I think my song has lasted almost long enough,
The subject's interesting, but rhymes are mighty rough;
I wish this war was over, when free from rags and fleas,
We'd kiss our wives and sweethearts, and gobble goober peas!

The Little Brown Jug

2

It's you who makes my friends my foes,
It's you who makes me wear old clothes;
Here you are so near my nose,
So tip her up and down she goes.

3

If I'd a cow that gave such milk,
I'd dress her in the finest silk;
I'd feed her on the choicest hay
And milk her forty times a day.

4

When I go toiling to my farm,
I take little brown jug under my arm;
I place it under a shady tree,
Little brown jug, it's you and me.

5

If all the folks in Adam's race,
Were gathered together in one place,
Then I'd prepare to shed a tear
Before I'd part from you, my dear.

6

The rose is red, my nose is too,
The violet's blue and so are you,
And yet I guess before I stop
We'd better take another drop.

Rye Whisky

With a slight drag

I'll eat when I'm hung-ry, I'll drink when I'm dry; If the

hard times don't kill me, I'll live till I die.

Chorus:

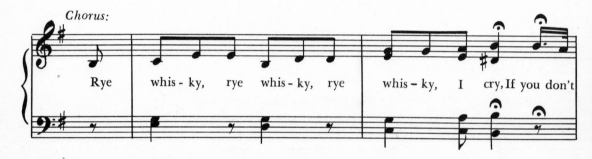

Rye whis - ky, rye whis - ky, rye whis - ky, I cry, If you don't

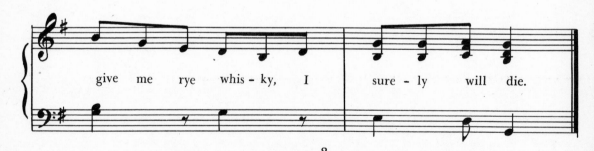

give me rye whis - ky, I sure - ly will die.

2

Beefsteak when I'm hungry, red liquor when I'm dry,
Greenbacks when I'm hard up, and religion when I die.

3

Sometimes I drink whisky, sometimes I drink rum,
Sometimes I drink brandy, at other times none.

4

But if I get boozy, my whisky's my own,
And them that don't like me can leave me alone.

5

Jack o' diamonds, Jack o' diamonds, I know you of old,
You've robbed my poor pockets of silver and gold.

6

If the ocean was whisky and I was a duck,
I'd dive to the bottom to get one sweet suck.

7

Oh, whisky, you villain, you've been my downfall,
You've kicked me, you've cuffed me—but I love you for all.

8

I'll drink my own whiskey, I'll drink my own wine;
Some ten thousand bottles I've killed in my time.

9

I've no wife to quarrel, no babies to bawl;
The best way of living is no wife at all.

10

You may boast of your knowledge and brag of your sense;
'Twill all be forgotten a hundred years hence.

Menagerie

Gaily

Van - burgh is the man who goes to all the shows, He goes in - to the li – on's den and tells you all he knows. He

sticks his head in-to the li-on's mouth and

keeps it there a while, And

when he takes it out a — gain, he

Chorus:

greets you with a smile. The

ele - phant now goes 'round, the band be - gins to play The boys a - round the mon - keys' cage had bet - ter keep a - way.

2

First comes the African Polar Bear, oft called the Iceberg's
    daughter,
She's been known to eat three tubs of ice, then call for soda
    water;
She wades in water up to her knees, not fearing any harm,
And you may grumble all you please, and she don't care a darn.

3

That hyena in the next cage, most wonderful to relate,
Got awful hungry the other day, ate up his female mate;
He's a very ferocious beast, don't go near him little boys,
For when he's mad he shakes his tail, and makes an awful noise.

4

Next comes the vulture, awful bird, from the mountain's highest
    tops,
He's been known to eat up little girls and then to lick his chops;
Oh, the show it can't go on, there's too much noise and con-
    fusion,
Oh, ladies, stop feeding those monkeys peanuts, it'll injure their
    constitution.

5

Next comes the Anaconda Boa Constrictor, oft called Anaconda
    for brevity,
He's noted the world throughout for his age and great longevity;
He can swallow himself, crawl through himself, and come out
    again with facility,
He can tie himself up with a double bow knot with his tail, and
    wink with the greatest agility.

The Man on the Flying Trapeze

Waltz time

Once I was hap-py but now I'm for-lorn

Like an old coat that is tat-tered and torn,

Left in this wide world fret and to mourn,

Be-tray'd by a maid in her teens

Now this girl that I loved, she was hand-some,

And I tried all I knew her to please

But I nev-er could please her one quar-ter so

well Like that man on the fly-ing tra-peze

Chorus:

He flies through the air with the great-est of

ease This dar-ing young man on the fly-ing tra-

peze. His move—ments are grace-ful, the girls he does

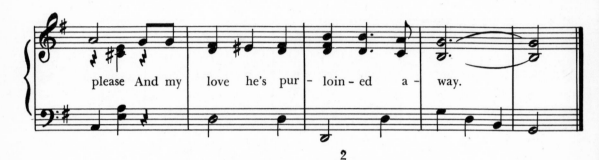

please And my love he's pur - loin - ed a - way.

2

This young man by name was Senor Boris Slang
Tall, big and handsome, as well made as Chang.
Whene'er he appeared the hall loudly rang
With ovation from all people there.
He'd smile from the bar on the people below,
And one night he smiled on my love.
She winked back at him and she shouted bravo
As he hung by his nose up above—

3

Her father and mother were both on my side
And tried very hard to make her my own bride.
Her father he sighed and her mother she cried
To see her throw herself away—
'Twas all no avail, she went there ev'ry night
And threw him bouquets on the stage
Which caused her to meet him—how he ran me down!
To tell it would take a whole page.

4

One night as usual, went to her dear home
Found there her mother and father alone.
I asked for my love, and soon 'twas made known
To my horror that she'd run away.
She packed up her boxes and eloped in the night
With him with the greatest of ease.
From two stories high he had lowered her down
To the ground on his flying trapeze.

5

Some months after that I went into a hall
To my surprise I found there on the wall
A bill in red letters which did my heart gall
That she was appearing with him—
He'd taught her gymnastics and dressed her in tights
To help him to live at his ease.
He'd made her assume a masculine name
And now she goes on the trapeze.

Last Chorus:
She floats through the air with the greatest of ease
You'd think her a man on the flying trapeze.
She does all the work while he takes his ease,
And that's what's become of my love—

The Animal Fair

Easy gait

I went to the an - im - al fair, The birds and the beasts were there; The old rac- coon By the light of the moon Was combing his gold – en hair. The monk - ey he got drunk And climbed up the elephant's trunk. The el- e - phant sneezed And fell on his knees And

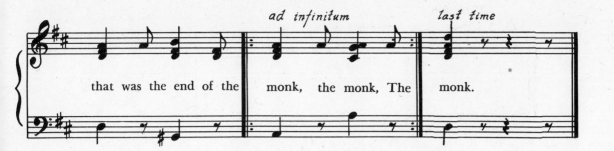

that was the end of the monk, the monk, The monk.

Lardy Dah

Chorus:

He wears a pen-ny flow-er in his coat, Lar-dy dah! And a pen-ny pap-er col-lar round his throat, Lar-dy dah! In his hand a pen-ny stick, in his mouth a quill tooth-pick. Not a pen-ny in his pock-et, Lar-dy dah! Lar-dy dah! Not a pen-ny in his pock-et, Lar-dy dah!

245

2

He is in a downtown office, Lardy dah! Lardy dah!
And he's quite a city toff, is Lardy dah!
He cuts a swell so fine,
And he quite forgets to dine
Unless he a friend can find, Lardy dah! Lardy dah!
As to pay for hash and wine, Lardy dah!

3

His shirt is very tricky, Lardy dah! Lardy dah!
It's a pair of cuffs and dickey, Lardy dah!
His boots are patent leather
But they never stand the weather
For they're paper glued together, Lardy dah! Lardy dah!
For they're paper stuck together, Lardy dah!

4

His bogus diamonds glitter, Lardy dah! Lardy dah!
But the girls all smile and titter, Lardy dah!
If he stays out late at night, ah,
And comes home rather tight, ah,
And his luncheon's very light, ah, Lardy dah! Lardy dah!
And this city swell so slight, ah, Lardy dah!

Champagne Charlie

Music by Alfred Lee

Rather strutting rhythm,

Of gai - et - y I've seen a deal through - out my boisterous life, But with all my grand ac - com - plish - ments I've ne'er ob - tained a wife. The thing I mostly ex - cel in is the "mid - night sup - per game," A noise all night, in bed all day, and swim - ming in cham - pagne.

Chorus:

For Champagne Charlie is my name— Champagne Charlie is my name Good for an-y game at night, my boys, Good for an-y game at night, my boys, Cham-pagne Char-lie is my name Cham-pagne Char-lie is my name Good for an-y game at night, boys! Who'll come and join me in a spree?

Where pleasures reign in cafés fine and hotels grand I dwell,
The girls on seeing me exclaim, "Oh, what a champagne swell!"
The notion 'tis of ev'ry one that if 'twere not for my name
And causing so much to be drunk, they'd never make cham-
    pagne.

3

The way I gained my title's by a fashion which I've got
Of never letting others pay, however long's the shot;
For whoe'er drinks at my expense is treated all the same,
"Fifth Avenue" or "Bowery style," I make them take champagne.

4

Some epicures like Burgundy, Hock, Claret and Moselle,
But 'tis Moet's vintage only satisfies this champagne swell!
What matter if to bed I go with head all muddled thick?
A "champagne" in the morning sets me "all right" very quick.

5

Perhaps you fancy what I say is nothing more than chaff,
And only told like other jokes to merely raise a laugh!
But let me prove I'm not in jest: I'll stand a bottle of "cham"
For each man round! Yes, that I will, and stand it like a lamb.

Josephus Orange Blossom

"Schottische" or "Barn Dance" time

My name it is Jos-eph-us Or-ange Blos-som. I'm the
When first I fell in love with Jane Mel-is-ser I

gay-est col-ored ge'm' man in the land; With the
tried my best to win from her a smile, I

pret-ty girls I al-ways play the pos-sum, I'm a
caught her round the waist and tried to kiss her, Says she,

'red-hot hun-ky dor-y con-tra-band.
"Go way, I does-n't like your style."

Guess not . . . Red - hot! . . . I'm the

gay - est col - or'd ge'm' man in the land, Oh! My name it is Jos-eph-us Or - ange Blos - som, I'm a red - hot hun -ky dor - y con - tra - band.

2

I tho't my Jane Melisser was a beauty
So I popped the question to her Sunday night;
Says she, "I think you are the one to suit me,
Your company always gives delight."
I told her that I tho't she was perfection,
Upon her charming face my eyes could feast,
And if she had no serious objection
Next Sunday night we'd patronize the priest.
Wasn't she sweet?—Hard to beat—
She was the blithest creature in the land,
And I knows she loves Josephus Orange Blossom.
I'm a red-hot hunky-dory contraband.

3

One evening sweet tho'ts were o'er me creeping;
I tho't upon my sweetheart I would call;
As in her window slyly I was peeping,
I saw something that did my heart appall:
Her teeth and one eye laid upon the table,
Her pretty curls were hanging on a peg.
I laughed aloud as hard as I was able,
To see her taking off a wooden leg.
Oh—no!—Not for Joe.—
No I can't take Melisser for a wife,
No!—So out of town I soon got up and dusted,
I never was so sold in all my life.

Cousin Jedediah

By H. S. Thompson

Briskly

Now, Jac - ob, get the cows home and put them in the pen, For the

cous - ins are a - com in' for to see us all a - gain; The

dow - dy's in the pan and the tur - key's on the fire, And we

all must get read - y for cous - in Jed - e - di - ah.

Chorus:

Cous - in Jed - ed - i - ah There's Hez - ek - i - ah and Az - ar - iah and

Aunt Soph-i-a and Jed-ed-iah, Oh, won't we have a jol - ly time, a jol - ly time, Jer - ush-a put the ket-tle on we'll all have tea.

2

Now Obed, wash your face, boy, and tallow up your shoes,
While I go to see Aunt Betty and tell her all the news;
And Kitty slick your hair and put on your Sunday gown,
For Cousin Jedediah comes right from Boston town.

3

Now Job, you peel the onions and wash and fix the taters,
We'll have them at the table in shiny painted waiters;
Put on your bran' new boots and those trousers with the straps,
Aunt Sophia'll take a shine to you if you look real slick, perhaps.

4

Tell Josh to put the colt in the double seated shay
Let him just card down the cattle, give them a little hay;
I'll wear my nice new bell-crown I bought of old Uriah,
And I guess we'll astonish our Cousin Jedediah.

Reuben and Rachel

Gaily, may be sung as a round

Words by Harry Birch
Music by William Gooch

Reu-ben, I have long been think-ing, What a good world
Rach-el, I have long been think-ing, What a fine world

this might be If the men were all trans-port-ed
this might be If we had some more young lad-ies

Far be-yond the North-ern Sea.
On this side the North-ern Sea.

1, 2.

last ending

2

Reuben, I'm a poor lone woman
No one seems to care for me, I
Wish the men were all transported
Far beyond the Northern Sea.

I'm a man without a victim,
Soon I think there's one will be
If the men are not transported
Far beyond the Northern Sea.

3

Reuben, what's the use of fooling,
Why not come up like a man?
If you'd like to have a "lover"
I'm for life your "Sally Ann!"

Oh my goodness, oh my gracious!
What a queer world this would be,
If the men were all transported
Far beyond the Northern Sea!

4

Reuben, now do stop your teasing
If you've any love for me;
I was only just a fooling,
As I thought of course you'd see.

Rachel, I will not transport you,
But will take you for a wife,
We will live on "milk and honey."
Better or worse, we're in for life.

Jeff in Petticoats

Music by
George Cooper

Words by
Henry Tucker

Jeff Dav-is was a he-ro bold, you've heard of him, I know, He tried to make him-self a King where south-ern breez-es blow; But "Unc-le Sam," he laid the youth a-cross his might-y knee, And spanked him well, and that's the end of brave old Jef-fy D.

Chorus:

Oh! Jef-fy D.! You "flow'r of chi-val-ree," Oh

roy - al   Jef — fy   D.! . . .   Your

Em - pire's but   a   tin - clad skirt, oh,   charm-ing Jef-fy   D.

2

This Davis, he was always full of bluster and of brag,
He swore, on all our Northern walls he'd plant his rebel rag;
But when to battle he did go, he said, "I'm not so green,
To dodge the bullets, I will wear my tin-clad crinoline."

3

Now when he saw the game was up, he started for the woods,
His band-box hung upon his arm quite full of fancy goods:
Said Jeff, "They'll never take me now, I'm sure I'll not be seen.
They'd never think to look for me beneath my crinoline."

4

Jeff took with him, the people say, a mine of golden coin,
Which he from banks and other places, managed to purloin:
But while he ran, like every thief, he had to drop the spoons,
And maybe that's the reason why he dropped his pantaloons!

5

Our Union boys were on his track for many nights and days,
His palpitating heart it beat, enough to burst his stays,
O! what a dash he must have cut with form so tall and lean;
Just fancy now the "What is it," dressed up in Crinoline!

6

The ditch that Jeff was hunting for, he found was very near;
He tried to "shift" his base again, his neck felt rather queer;
Just on the out-"skirts" of a wood his dainty shape was seen,
His boots stuck out, and now they'll hang old Jeff in Crinoline.

Kingdom Comin'

By Henry C. Work

With spirit

Stacc.

Say dark-eys hab you seen de mas-sa wid de mus-tash on his face, Go long de road some-time dis mor-nin' like he gwine to leab de place? He seen a smoke way up de ribber where de Lin-kum gun-boats lay, He took his hat an' lef' ber-ry sud-den an' I spec de's run a-

2

He six foot one way, two foot tudder, and he weigh tree hundred
    pound,

His coat so big he couldn't pay de tailor an' it won't go half way
    round.

He drill so much dey call him Cap'an an' he get so drefful tann'd,

I spect he try an' fool dem Yankees for to tink he's contraband.

3

De darkeys feel so lonesome living in de log house on de lawn,
Dey move deir tings to massa's parlor for to keep it while he's
    gone.
Dar's wine an' cider in de kitchen an' de darkeys dey'll hab some;
I spose dey'll all be confiscated when de Linkum sojers come.

4

De oberseer he make us trouble an' he drive us round a spell;
We lock him up in de smoke house cellar wid de key trown in de
    well.
De whip is lost, de hancuff broken, but de massa'll hab his pay;
He's ole enough, big enough, ought to know better dan to went
    an' run away.

Musieu Bainjo

With a jaunty air

Voy – ez   ce mu – let   là,   Mu – sieu Bain –jo
Look at   that dark – ey,   Mis   –   ter   Ban – jo

Comme il   est in – so   – lent!   Cha – peau sur co –
Does – n't   he put on   airs!   Walk – ing stick in

té, Musieu Bain – jo,   La   canne a   la   main, Musieu Bain – jo,
hand, Mis – ter Ban – jo,   Hat   cocked on   one   side, Mis – ter Ban – jo,

Bottes qui   fait   crin –   crin, Musieu Bain – jo   Voy – ez   ce mu – let
Boots that   go   "crank –   crank," Mister Ban – jo   Look at   that darkey

la, Mu – sieu Bain – jo   Comme il   est in – so –   lent!
there, Mis – ter Ban – jo   Does – n't   he put   on   airs!

261

Words and music
by Eastburn

Oil on the Brain

Probably a pseudonym
for J. E. Winner

The Yan-kees boast that they make clocks Which just beat all cre-

a - tion, They nev - er made one could keep time With our great spec-ul-

a - tion. Our stocks like clocks go with a spring, Wind up run down a-

gain: But all our *strikes* are sure to cause Oil on the brain.

Chorus:

Stock's par, stock's up, Then on the wane;

Ev'- ry -bod -y's troub-led with Oil on the brain.

2

There's various kinds of oil afloat,
Cod liver, Castor, Sweet;
Which tend to make a sick man *well*
And set him on his *feet*.
But one a curious feat performs,
We just a *well* obtain,
And set the people crazy with
Oil on the brain.

3

There's neighbor Smith, a poor young man,
Who couldn't raise a dime;
Had clothes which boasted many rents,
And took his "nip" on time.
But now he's clad in dandy style,
Sports diamonds, kids and cane;
And his success was owing to
Oil on the brain.

4

Miss Simple drives her coach and four
And dresses in high style:
And Mr. Shoddy courts her strong
Because her "Dad's struck ile."
Her jewels, laces, velvets, silks
Of which she is so vain
Were bought by Dad the time he had
Oil on the brain.

5

The lawyers, doctors, hatters, clerks,
Industrious and lazy,
Have put their money all in stocks,
In fact have gone oil crazy.
They'd better stick to briefs and pills,
Hot irons, ink and pen;
Or they will kick the bucket from
Oil on the brain.

6

There's Maple Shad, Excelsior,
Bull Creek, Big Tank, Dalcell;
And Keystone, Star, Venango Briggs,
Organic and Farrell.
Petroleum, Saint Nicolas,
Corn Planter, New Creek vein;
Sure 'tis no wonder many have
Oil on the brain.

Ballad of the Boll Weevil

With an easy swing

Oh have you heard de lat-est De lat-es' of the songs? It's a-bout dem lit-tle Boll Wee-vils Dey's picked up bofe feet and gone, A-lookin' for a home Jes' a-lookin' for a home.

2
De Boll Weevil is a little bug
From Mexico dey say;
He come to try dis Texas soil
En thought he'd better stay,
A-lookin' for a home—
Jes' a-lookin' for a home.

264

3

First time I saw de Boll Weevil
He wuz on the western plain;
Next time I saw him
He was ridin' a Memphis train,
A-lookin' for a home—
Jes' a-lookin' for a home.

4

De fust time I saw de Boll Weevil
He wuz settin' on de square;
De nex' time I saw de Boll Weevil
He had all his family dere,
A-lookin' for a home—
Jes' a-lookin' for a home.

5

De farmer took de Boll Weevil
An' put him in de sand;
De Boll Weevil say to de farmer
"I'll stan' it like a man.
For it is my home.
It is my home."

6

Then the farmer got angry,
Sent him up in a balloon;
"Good bye Mr. Farmer,
I'll see you again next June,"
A-lookin' for a home—
Jes' a-lookin' for a home.

7

Den de farmer took de Boll Weevil,
An' lef' him on de ice.
Says de Boll Weevil to de farmer
"Dis mighty cool an' nice,"
Oh it is my home—
It is my home.

8

Mr. Farmer took little weevil
And put him in Paris Green;
"Thank you, Mr. Farmer,
It's the best I ever seen,"
It's my home—
It is my home.

9

Den de farmer say to the merchant
"We's in a awful fix;
De Boll Weevil's et all de cotton up
An' lef' us only sticks.
We's got no home—
Oh, we's got no home."

10

Oh de farmer say to de merchant
"I ain't made but one bale,
An' befo' I bring yo' dat one
I'll fight an' go to jail."
I'll have a home—
I'll have a home.

11

De Boll Weevil say to de farmer
"You better lemme alone
I've et up all yo' cotton
An' now I'll begin on de co'n."
I'll have a home—
I'll have a home.

12

Boll Weevil say to de doctor
"Better po' out all yo' pills,
When I get through wid de farmer
He cain't pay no doctor's bills,"
He'll have no home—
He'll have no home.

13

De merchant got half de cotton
De Boll Weevil got de rest.
Didn't leave de nigger's wife
But one old cotton dress
And it's full of holes,
Oh, it's full of holes.

Darky Sunday School

Fast

The earth was made in six days and fin – ished on the seventh, Ac – cord – ing to the con – tract it should have been the 'leventh. The car – pen – ters got drunk and the mas – ons would – n't work, So the cheap – est thing to do was to fill it up with dirt.

Chorus: Old folks, young folks, ev – ery – bod – y come, Join the dark – ies' Sun – day school and make your – selves to home. Kind – ly check your chew – ing gum and raz – ors at the door, And we'll tell you Bib – le stor – ies that you nev – er heard be – fore.

2

Adam was the first man and Eve she was his spouse;
They lost their job for stealing fruit and went to keeping house.
All was very peaceful and quiet on the main
Until a little baby came and they started raising Cain.

3

Cain he raised potatoes and he peddled them in town.
Abel called him hayseed every time he came around.
Cain he laid a stick of wood on brother Abel's head,
And when he took that stick away, he found poor Abel dead.

4

Noah was a mariner who sailed around the sea,
With half a dozen wives and a big menagerie;
He failed the first season when it rained for forty days,
For in that sort of weather no circus ever pays.

5

Methuselah is famous, because he couldn't croak,
Although he finally grew to be an old and seedy bloke.
He had so many whiskers that you couldn't see his head;
If he'd lived a little longer, he'd have used them for his bed.

6

Jonah was an emigrant, so runs the Bible tale,
He took an ocean voyage in a transatlantic whale.
The whale was overcrowded and Jonah was distressed,
So Jonah pushed the button and the whale did all the rest.

7

David was a shepherd's boy, his mother's pride and joy;
His father gave him a slingshot, a harmless little toy.
Along came Goliath, a-looking for a fuss,
David heaved a cobblestone and busted in his crust.

8

Samson was a strong man of the John L. Sullivan school;
He killed a thousand Philistines with the jawbone of a mule!
Along came a woman who filled him up with gin,
And shaved off his whiskers and the coppers pulled him in.

For Men Only

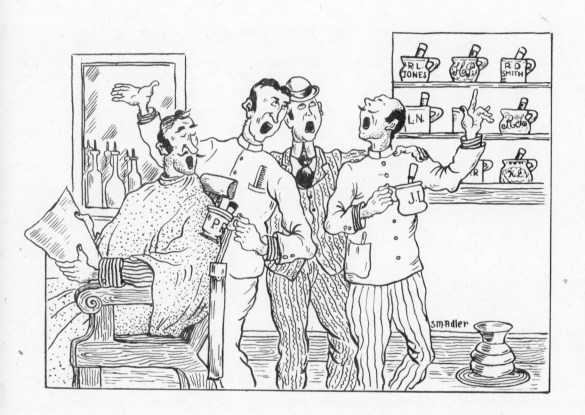

IN THE PAST AMERICAN MEN HAVE BEEN SHY IN
queer ways. They have tended to deprecate noisy, overwrought out-
bursts of emotion; shrieks of joy, extravagant words like "divine" and
"adore" they consider to be female in spirit. Eloquence they admired,

269

but mistrust; the bumbling dullard at the directors' meeting is more likely to arouse the stockholders' confidence than the smooth expounder of well-formed propositions. Glib, plausible, well-delivered talk arouses images of actors, circus hawkers and other impostors. Music they secretly enjoyed, but considered it to be unmanly.

But on occasion, these same men thaw out very nicely. Get them together in friendly assembly, away from the embarrassing presence of women or children, in club houses, gym lockers, camping trips, or saloons, pour a little liquor under their waists and unsuspected lyrical resources may be tapped. A charming sentiment will come to expression, good harmony will develop, with sweetly sliding progressions and poignant dissonances.

Why this sort of thing is called "barber shop" is something of a mystery. In that remote planet that those of us who were alive before 1914 used to inhabit, there were certain places sacred and inviolate to the use of men. No petticoats ever imaginably rustled inside of polling booths, saloons or barber shops. But of these the most immovably masculine was the barber shop. Women openly aspired to the vote, and were encouraged to do so by many men; on some social levels family women might still respectably enter the rear portions of saloons to "rush the growler," but no one could envisage, if ever so dreamily, multitudes of females demanding hair-cuts and shaves. A barber shop was always a rather unlikely place for a quartet, but perhaps its ancient uncompromising maleness made it seem a good metaphor for male music.

"Barber shop" is not primarily humorous; indeed most of the old favorites, such as "Sweet Adeline" and "By the Old Mill Stream" are heavily sentimental. Yet in recent years a tendency to parody this

270

same sentiment is much in evidence. "It's the Syme the 'Ole World Over" seems too pat to be genuine Cockney, it has the flavor of burlesque. "Lydia Pinkham" goes very well in 4/4 time, and may be hiked to.

The song "The Billboard" is chiefly heard around boys' camps and schools. Its items establish it pretty well as dating from about 1910 or earlier. Are there many people too young to know that Lillian Russell was a famous and pulchritudinous actress, that Cascarets were a tablet laxative, Sapolio a gritty household cleanser sold in cakes, Shinola a shoe-polish, and that Chauncey M. Depew was a well-known New York Central Railroad attorney and state politician, who told so many good stories that people assumed he told them all?

Clementine

In measured rhythm, not fast

Words and music
by Percy Montrose

In a cav - ern, in a can - yon, ex - cav - at - ing for mine, Dwelt a min - er, a for - ty - nin - er, and his daugh-ter Clem - ent- ine.

Refrain:

Oh my dar - ling, oh my dar - ling, oh my

dar - ling Clem-ent - ine, You are lost and gone for -

ev - er, dref - ful sor - ry, Clem - ent - ine.

2

Light she was and like a fairy, and her shoes were number nine;
Herring boxes without topses sandals were for Clementine.

3

Drove she ducklings to the water every morning just at nine,
Hit her foot against a splinter, fell into the foaming brine.

4

Ruby lips above the water, blowing bubbles soft and fine,
Alas for me! I was no swimmer, so I lost my Clementine.

5

In a churchyard near the canyon, where the myrtle doth entwine,
There grow roses and other posies, fertilized by Clementine.

6

Then the miner, forty-niner, soon began to peak and pine,
Thought he oughter jine his daughter, now he's with his Clementine.

7

In my dreams she still doth haunt me, robed in garments soaked
in brine,
Though in life I used to hug her, now she's dead I'll draw the
line.

Abdul Abulbul Amir

Waltz time

The sons of the Proph-et are brave men and bold, And quite un-ac-cust-omed to fear, But the brav-est by far in the ranks of the Shah, Was Ab-dul Ab-ul-bul Am-ir.

2

If you wanted a man to encourage the van
Or harass the foe from the rear,
Storm fort or redoubt, you had only to shout
For Abdul Abulbul Amir.

3

Now the heroes were plenty and well known to fame
In the troops that were led by the Czar,
And the bravest of these was a man by the name
Of Ivan Skavinsky Skavar.

274

4

He could jump fifty yards and tell fortunes at
    cards
And strum on the Spanish guitar,
In fact quite the cream of this Muscovite team
Was Ivan Skavinsky Skavar.

5

One day this bold Russian, he shouldered his
    gun
And donned his most truculent sneer,
Downtown he did go where he trod on the
    toe
Of Abdul Abulbul Amir.

6

"Young man," quoth Abdul, "has life grown
    so dull
That you wish to end your career?
Vile infidel, know, you have trod on the toe
Of Abdul Abulbul Amir!"

7

"So take your last look at sunshine and brook
And send your regrets to the Czar—
For by this I imply, you are going to die,
Count Ivan Skavinsky Skavar!"

8

Then this bold Mameluke drew his trusty
    skibouk,
Singing "Allah Il Allah! Al-lah!"
And with murderous intent he ferociously
    went,
For Ivan Skavinsky Skavar.

9

They parried and thrust, they side-stepped
    and cussed,
Of blood they spilled a great part;
The philologist blokes, who seldom crack
    jokes,
Say that hash was first made on that spot.

10

They fought all that night 'neath the pale
    yellow moon;
The din, it was heard from afar,
And huge multitudes came, so great was the
    fame,
Of Abdul and Ivan Skavar.

11

As Abdul's long knife was extracting the life,
In fact he was shouting "Huzzah!
He felt himself struck by the wily Calmuck,
Count Ivan Skavinsky Skavar.

12

The Sultan drove by in his red-breasted fly,
Expecting the victor to cheer,
But he only drew nigh to hear the last sigh
Of Abdul Abulbul Amir.

13

There's a tomb rises up where the Blue
    Danube rolls,
And 'graved there in characters clear,
Is, "Stranger, when passing, oh pray for the
    soul
Of Abdul Abulbul Amir."

14

A splash in the Black Sea one dark moonless night
Caused ripples to spread wide and far,
It was made by a sack fitting close to the back
Of Ivan Skavinsky Skavar.

15

A Muscovite maiden her lone vigil keeps
'Neath the light of the cold northern star,
And the name that she murmurs in vain as she weeps,
Is "Ivan Skavinsky Skavar."

The Billboard

As I was walk-ing down the street A bill-board met my eye; The ad-ver-tise-ments writ-ten there Would make you laugh and cry. The wind and rain had come that day And washed it half a-way, And what was left up-on that sign Would make that bill-board say:

2

Come smoke a Coca-Cola,
Chew catsup cigarettes,
See Lillian Russell wrestle
With a box of Cascarets;
Good pork and beans will meet tonight
In a finish fight.
Chauncey Depew will lecture
On Sapolio tonight.

3

Bay rum is good for horses,
It is the best in town;
Castoria cures the measles
You pay five dollars down.
Teeth extracted without pain
For the price of half a dime,
Overcoats are selling now
A little out of time.

4

Chew Wrigley's for that headache,
Take Campbell's for that cough,
There's going to be a swimming meet
In the village watering trough.
Buy a case of ginger ale,
It makes the best of broth,
Shinola's sure to curl the hair
And not to take it off.

The Dog-Catcher's Child

Slowly, with "feeling"

Oh, the moon shines to-night on the riv - er, But not on the dog - catch-er's child, For he fed her some raw liv - er, And raw meat makes dog - peop-le wild; Now he

It's the Syme the 'Ole World Over

Slowly, dolefully

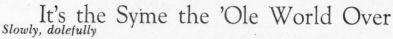

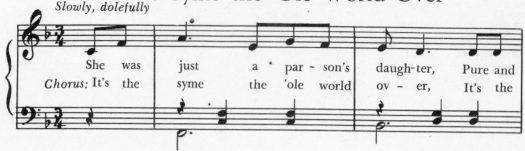

She was just a par-son's daugh-ter, Pure and
Chorus: It's the syme the 'ole world ov - er, It's the

un - styned was her nyme, First 'e 'ad 'er then 'e
poor what tykes the blyme; It's the rich what gets the

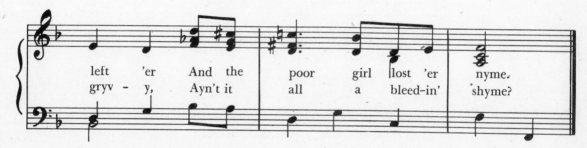

left 'er And the poor girl lost 'er nyme.
gryv - y, Ayn't it all a bleed-in' shyme?

2
Then she went to London city,
For to 'ide 'er 'orrid shyme;
There she met another squire,
Once agyne she lost 'er nyme.

3
Look at 'im with all 'is 'orses,
Drinking champygne in 'is club;
While the victim of 'is passions
Drinks her Guinness in a pub.

4
'Ear 'im in the 'Ouse of Commons,
Mykin' laws to put down crime;
While the womyun that 'e ruined
'Angs 'er 'ead in wicked shyme.

5
See 'er in 'er 'orse and carriage
Drivin' dyly through the park;
Though she's myde a wealthy marriage,
Still she 'ides a brykin' 'eart.

6
In their poor and 'umble dwelling,
Where 'er grievin' parents live;
Drinkin' champygne that she's sent 'em,
But they never can forgive.

7
In a rose embowered cottage
There was born a child of sin.
But the byby had no father
So she gently did 'im in.

Lydia Pinkham

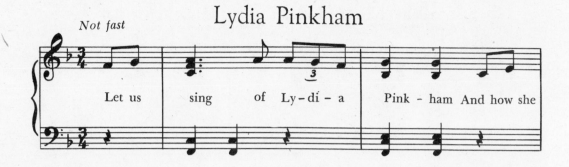

Not fast

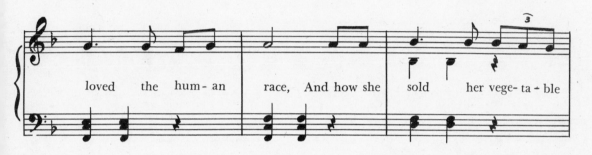

Let us sing of Ly-di-a Pink-ham And how she

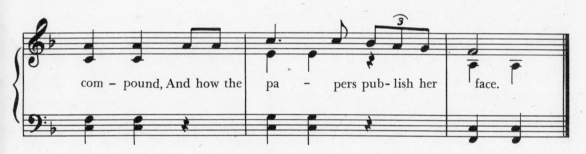

loved the hum-an race, And how she sold her vege-ta-ble

com-pound, And how the pa - pers pub-lish her face.

2

Oh Mrs. Brown could do no housework
Oh Mrs. Brown could do no housework
She took three bottles of Lydia's compound,
Now there's nothing she will shirk!

3

Mrs. Jones she had no children
And she loved them very dear;
So she took six bottles of Pinkham's—
Now she has twins every year.

4

Lottie Smyth ne'er had a lover,
Blotchy pimples caused her plight;
But she took nine bottles of Pinkham's—
Sweethearts swarm about her every night.

One More Drink for the Four of Us

four   of   us. Sing   glor – y be   to hob there's no

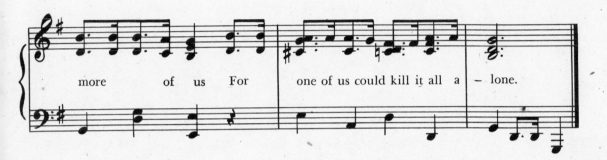

more   of us For   one of us could kill it all a – lone.

To the Tune Of

Father, dear Father —

A PARODY IS SORT OF CARICATURE, BUT IT USES
a song for its model instead of a person or object. Its humorous quality
will, of course, depend on whether the parodied song is already familiar. If it is not, the point is largely lost.

All American songs, if they come to be widely sung for a sufficient length of time, tend to get themselves parodied. It is a sort of tribute that Americans pay to their songs, thus to maul them affectionately. But as often as not, it is a serious or heavily sentimental song that is parodied into flippancy. Again the American sense of humor insists on limiting excessive emotional pretensions.

It is always the words that are parodied; the music is left intact. Purely tonal parody is appreciated only by experienced musicians. Parody must be distinguished as carefully as may be from the common practice of singing new words to old tunes. The latter is merely a makeshift due to a poverty of musical thought. It may turn out to be humorous, but it is still not a parody. A man may wear his father's old trousers because he has none of his own. It may look funny, but it is still not a caricature.

Most American parodies never see print. They are casually dished up at clubs, schools, amateur shows, etc.

The songs here reproduced are all distortions of famous sentimental songs of the middle of the last century. "Barber, Spare Those Hairs" is fashioned after George P. Morris's and Henry Russel's "Woodman, Spare That Tree." It was done by John Love, New York University, class of 1868. "Father, Dear Father, Come Down with the Stamps" takes off the famous temperance song "Father, Dear Father, Come Home, The Clock on the Steeple Struck One," by Henry C. Work, frequently sung during the play, 'Ten Nights in a Bar-Room.' It appeared in 1867, a few years after the original.

"Bacon on the Rind" may not be immediately recognized as a parody by some people. The fame of the original has paled somewhat. It caricatures the once well-known heart-rending poem "Bingen on

285

the Rhine." Only this time the dying soldier is sending word to his loved ones far away that it was the army food that got him. It was done in the army, probably in the Philippines.

"Pie in the Sky" is a rather acrid left flank attack on the intimations of immortality contained in the formerly popular song "In the Sweet By and By."

"Father, Dear Father" may need a glossary. "Stamps" here do not mean certificates of postage prepayment. For a few years after the Civil War the word was used colloquially to indicate printed paper currency. So "Stamps" means money. "Stewart's" is A. T. Stewart, the famous New York store, predecessor of Wanamaker's. "Waterfall" was a form of feminine hair-do, fashionable in the 1860's and later. Apparently a ledge of solid foreign matter was cunningly smuggled under the tresses, allowing them to describe a graceful parabola. "Braiteau" seems to have been a New York hairdresser.

Father, Dear Father, Come Down with the Stamps

Moderato

Music by Frank Wilder

O fath - er, dear fath - er, come down with the stamps, My

dress - mak - er's bill is un - paid

said she would send it right home from the shop As

soon as the floun-ces were made. Come

down, come down, come down! Please

fath - er, dear fath - er, come down!

Chorus:

O, hear the sweet voice of thy child, Who

cries in her room all a - lone, ... Oh,

who could re - sist her most   pit - i - ful tears So

fath - er,   with stamps quick come   down!

2

My new dress from Stewart's is down in the hall,
The boy will not leave it without pay
I've nothing to sport with—can't go to the ball,
So please send the shop-boy away!
Come down, come down, come down!
Please father, dear father, come down!

3

The hair-dresser said he would not do them up,
My curls are not fit to be seen;
O father, dear father, come down with the stamps,
Unless I could pay him fifteen.
Come down, come down, come down!
Please father, dear father, come down!

4

He only asks twenty to give a new set,
And take the old hair in exchange;
Besides, pa, my waterfall's awfully rough,
And so my back hair will look strange.
Come down, come down, come down!
Please father for Braiteau, come down!

Barber, Spare Those Hairs

Words by
John Love
Music by Henry Russell

Slowly, with expression

O bar - ber, spare those hairs,

Which sprout from both my cheeks, A

sol - ace for my cares; I 've

cher - ished them for weeks. They

come in sin - gle file, As

though a - fraid to bloom; But

still they're all the style, So,

bar - ber, give them room.

2

I've reached a Junior's state,
Its dignity and fame;
And though these hairs came late,
They still can honor claim.
With awe the Freshmen see
These proofs of ripening years;
And bow while passing me,
Beset with trembling fears.

3

O, give them yet a year,
The strength'ning sap to draw;
For then you need not fear,
They'll grow two inches more.
Then, barber, list to me,
And bend unto my cry;
O, let my whiskers be,
Not yet thy calling ply.

4

And when I'm passing near,
'Twill be, I'm sure, no wrong,
Your waiting eyes to cheer
With whiskers thick and long.
Now, barber, fare thee well;
The blade put on its shelf,
And ne'er this story tell,
But keep it to yourself.

Bacon on the Rind

Slowly, with mock sentiment

A sol – dier in the cav – al – ry lay

on a can – vas bunk, On a soap – box there be-

side him lay a hunk of arm – y punk; And as he

chewed a – way and bus – y, his face turned ash – en

gray, For the sol – dier boy was dy – ing in the

Is - land far a - way.   As his   com - rades knelt be -

side him   to   hear   what he   might   say,   The

dy - ing sol - dier   fal — tered, "Bring   me a bunch of

hay,   For my   horse has   food   in   plen - ty, and the

grub is left be - hind,   And   I   must starve on

Bac - on, Arm - y   Bac - on   on   the   Rind."

rit.

293

2

And as he lay there gasping with the moments flying fast,
He tried to chew a rubber boot 'fore life went out at last.
And he said to his comrades, "Bring me a box of soap,
For they eat it in the frozen north, and where there is life
    there is hope.
But, Charlie dear, I greatly fear, my race is almost run,
Life's feeble spark will be snuffed out ere the setting of the sun.
Take a message and a token to the dear ones left behind,
And say I starved on Bacon, Army Bacon on the Rind."

3

That evening just at twilight, as the flag slid down the pole,
We bowed our heads in silence for the parting soul;
But that night beside the camp-fire you could hear his comrades
    say,
"If he's had a soldier's ration he'd be alive today.
A curse on the man who did it, tho' with coin his purse be lined,
May he starve on Prunes and Bacon, Army Bacon on the Rind."
In a trim New England cottage sits a mother old and gray.
In her hand she holds a letter that came by mail that day.

4

And as she sits there reading, her eyes are filled with tears,
For the letter brings the tidings that every mother fears.
It tells how in the Islands her darling met his death,
Fighting for flag and country midst the battle's frenzied breath;
But it don't tell how it happened, and perhaps the Fates are
    kind,
For her darling starved on Bacon, Army Bacon on the Rind.

Pie in the Sky

Words by Joe Hill

Long haired preach-ers come here ev-ery night And they tell you what's wrong and what's right. When you ask a - bout some - thing to eat, They will ans - wer with voic - es so sweet:

Chorus

You'll get pie, by and by, In that

Drink It Down

ONCE UPON A TIME, AMERICAN COLLEGES WERE
all male. So the atmosphere of their musical activities was a little like
that of the "barber shop" hereinbefore described. But there were essential differences. For one thing, the college boys were a good deal

297

younger, and enjoyed making more noise. They had a lot more songs that exuded loyalty to something or other, class, team or alma mater; and they enjoyed more songs with nonsense words. But still many college songs come to be "barber shop" items, many ditties were plied by both the young and the middle-aged indiscriminately.

Extensive collections of college songs were made toward the middle of the nineteenth century, and reveal that the boys were mostly willing to do their exuberating to borrowed tunes. However, the famous "Lone Fish-Ball," composed about 1854, seems to have been composed without carbon paper. Under the title is added the interesting information: "Founded on a Boston Fact." In "Carmina Collegiensia," one of the earliest anthologies, there is further appended an affecting tale of a New York professor, who made a nuisance of himself in his habitual restaurant because he always wanted more than one portion of three buckwheat cakes for six cents, but less than two portions for twelve. He insisted on five buckwheat cakes for ten cents, drove everybody wild and finally had to stay away from the restaurant altogether.

"Here's to Good Old Yale, Drink it Down, Drink it Down" likewise goes back to those days and has since been found acceptable to other colleges of monosyllabic name.

"Co-ca-che-lunk," they say, first started in the army, but the colleges did the most toward propagating it. It is an attractive tune, and the syllables of the refrain seem congruous with the barbaric yells with which they decorate their football games.

One of the sets of words of the song makes a mention of something that was once of great importance in the undergraduate world. Thirty years ago, average American youths were still being constrained

298

to go through the motions of being seventeeth century English gentlemen by trying to ingest the snarls and eddies of Latin and Greek sentence structure into their candid minds. Most of them succumbed to the corruption of using published translations done by experts. Such unethical but time-saving aid was called a "pony" a "horse" or "trot." Are they still in use today? (*Editor's note: Yes.*)

"Solomon Levi" seems to have appeared during the 1880's. The song has had several variants, chiefly concerning the name of the street where the famous second-hand clothing merchant is supposed to have had his premises. There is a Salem Street in Cambridge, but there seems to be no evidence that its number 149 ever harbored a Solomon Levi. On the other hand the song is sometimes sung "Chatham Street." But where is Chatham Street? One edition calles it "Baxter Street." This is likely enough New York address, but it is rather far away to have gotten any of the college trade.

One old Harvard graduate, indulging in reminiscences, talks of a merchant named Levi who was nicknamed the "Poco," who frequently visited the campus where his dignified bearded appearance caused him to be occasionally mistaken for a professor. But his aim was to sell pictures and other knick-knacks to students. Second handed clothing was another of his lines. There had been a hardly credible legend to the effect that he had once paid as much as five dollars for a new dress suit that had been ordered by a man who died before he could ever wear it. Perhaps this was the original of the renowned Solomon.

In recent years the colleges have become sophisticated; in fact they are almost becoming adult. Regular choral groups have gone highbrow, and have deserted the bull-dog on the bank for Palestrina.

299

Co-Ca-Che-Lunk

In march time

When we first came on this cam-pus, Freshmen we, as green as grass; Now, as grave and rev-erend sen — iors, Smile we ov-er the ver – dant past.

Chorus:

Co-ca-che-lunk-che- lunk – che-la – ly, Co- ca– che-lunk-che- lunk -che-lay, Co-ca-che-lunk-che- lunk – che-la – ly, Hi! O chick-a-che- lunk-che-lay.

2

We have fought the fight together,
We have struggled side by side;
Broken is the bond that held us—
We must cut our sticks and slide.

3

Some will go to Greece or Hartford,
Some to Norwich or to Rome;
Some to Greenland's icy mountains—
More, perhaps, will stay at home.

4

When we come again together,
Vigintennial to pass,
Wives and children all included—
Won't we be an uproarious class?

1

Tell me not in mournful numbers
Of long nights and weary toil;
Broken and uneasy slumbers,
And the wasting midnight oil.

2

Tell me not of unshorn whiskers
Of each gloomy sophomore
Contemplating Sophroniscus,
Cramming Euclid o'er and o'er

3

But we did not wander blindly
Through our Latin and our Greek;
Let us think a moment kindly
Of our quadrupeds so sleek.

4

Though our labors swiftly bore us
("Bore us" not as tutors do)
Singing here today our chorus.
Think we of our *ponies* too.

5

Bright the sky is beaming o'er us.
Fresh and Sophomore years are o'er;
Juniors join in singing chorus.
Sing "biennials are a bore."

The Lone Fish-Ball

Leisurely

There was a man went up and down To seek a

din-ner through the town. *Chorus:* There was a man went up and

down To seek a din-ner through the town.

2

What wretch is he who wife forsakes,
Who best of jam and waffles makes?

3

He feels his cash to know his pence,
And finds he has but just six cents.

4

He finds at last a right cheap place,
And enters in with modest face.

5

The bill-of-fare he searches through
To see what his six cents will do.

6

The cheapest viand of them all
Is "twelve and a half cents for two fish-balls."

7

The waiter he to him doth call
And gently whispers "One fish-ball."

8

The waiter roars it through the hall,
The guests they start at "One fish-ball!"

9

The guest then says, quite ill at ease,
"A piece of bread, sir, if you please."

10

The waiter roars it through the hall:
"We don't give bread with one fish-ball!"

MORAL
11

Who would have bread with his fish-ball
Must get it first or not at all.

12

Who would fish-ball with fixins eat,
Must get some friend to stand a treat.

Bingo

Lots of pep

Here's to good old Yale, drink it down, drink it down.

Here's to good old Yale, drink it down, drink it down.

Here's to good old Yale, she's so heart-y and so hale, Drink it

down, drink it down, drink it down, drink it down.

Fine

Balm of Gil-e-ad, Gil-e-ad. Balm of Gil-e-ad, Gil-e-ad.

Balm of Gil-e-ad, way down on the Bin-go farm. We

won't go home an-y more, We won't go home an-y more, We

won't go home an-y more, Way down on the Bin-go farm.

Bin-go, Bin-go, Bin-go, Bin-go, Bin-go, Bin-go Way

down on the Bin-go farm. *spoken* B - I - N - G - O

D. C. al Fine

The Bull Dog

307

2

Oh, the bull-dog stooped to catch him,
And the snapper caught his paw;
Oh, the bull-dog stooped to catch him,
And the snapper caught his paw;
Oh, the bull-dog stopped to catch him
And the snapper caught his paw,
The pollywog died a-laughing
To see him wag his jaw.

3

Says the monkey to the owl,
"Oh, what'll you have to drink?"
Says the monkey to the owl,
"Oh, what'll you have to drink?"
"Why since you are so very kind,
I'll take a bottle of ink."

4

Oh, the bull-dog in the yard,
And the tom-cat on the roof,
Oh, the bull-dog in the yard,
And the tom-cat on the roof,
Are practising the highland fling
And singing opera bouffe.

5

Says the tom-cat to the dog:
"Oh, set your ears agog,"
Says the tom-cat to the dog:
"Oh, set your ears agog,
For Julie's about to tete-a-tete
With Romeo incog."

6

Says the bull-dog to the cat:
"Oh, what do you think they're at?
Says the bull-dog to the cat:
"Oh, what do you think they're at?
They're spooning in the dead of night,
But where's the harm in that?"

7

Pharoah's daughter on the bank,
Little Moses in the pool,
Pharoah's daughter on the bank,
Little Moses in the pool,
She fished him out with a telegraph pole,
And sent him off to school.

Solomon Levi

By Fred Seaver

My name is So - lo - mon Le - vi, At my store on Sal - em street, That's where you'll buy your coats and vests And ev - 'ry - thing that's neat; I've sec - ond-hand - ed uls - ter - ettes And ev - 'ry - thing that's

fine,   For   all   the boys   they   trade with me   At a

hun – dred   and   for – ty – nine.

REFRAIN:

Oh,   So - lo - mon   Le – vi,   Le – vi,   tra la la   la!

Poor   sheen - y   Le – vi,

Tra la la la la la la la la la la, My name is So-lo-mon Le-vi, at my store on Sal-em street, That's where you'll buy your coats and vests and ev-ry-thing that's neat; Sec-ond-hand-ed

311

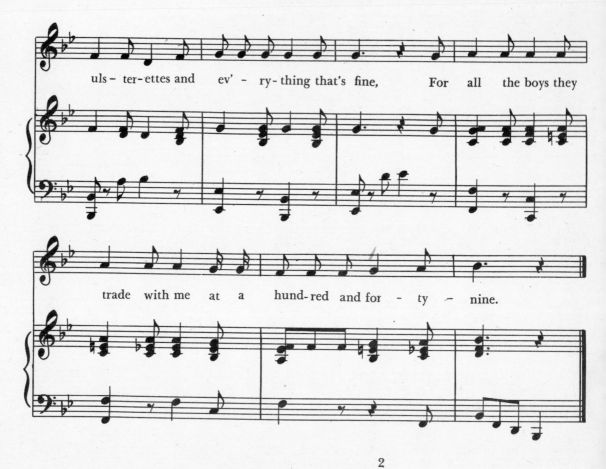

uls – ter–ettes and ev' – ry–thing that's fine, For all the boys they

trade with me at a hund-red and for – ty – nine.

2

And if a bummer comes along,
To my store on Salem street,
And tries to hang me up for coats
And vests so very neat,
I kicks the bummer right out of my store
And on him sets my pup,
For I won't sell clothing to any man
Who tries to set me up.

3

The people are delighted
To come inside my store,
And trade with the elegant gentleman
What I keeps to walk the floor;
He's a blood among the sheenies,
Beloved by one and all,
And his clothes they fit him just like
The paper on the wall.

Shool

With sprightly rhythm

I wish I was in Bos — ton Ci — ty Where all the girls they are so pret — ty, If I did — n't have a time 'twould be a pit — y — Dis — cum bib — le lol — la boo,

2

I wish I was on yonder hill,
For there I'd sit and cry my fill
And every drop should turn a mill—
Discum bible lolla boo, slow reel.

3

I wish I was a married man
And had a wife whose name was Fan,
I'd sing her a song on this same plan—
Discum bible lolia boo, slow reel.

INDEX

INDEX CONTINUED